Philosophy of Science
after Feminism

Studies in Feminist Philosophy is designed to showcase cutting-edge monographs and collections that display the full range of feminist approaches to philosophy, that push feminist thought in important new directions, and that display the outstanding quality of feminist philosophical thought.

STUDIES IN FEMINIST PHILOSOPHY
Cheshire Calhoun, *Series Editor*

Advisory Board

Published in the series:

Abortion and Social Responsibility: Depolarizing the Debate
Laurie Shrage

Gender in the Mirror: Confounding Imagery
Diana Tietjens Meyers

Autonomy, Gender, Politics
Marilyn Friedman

Setting the Moral Compass: Essays by Women Philosophers
Edited by Cheshire Calhoun

Burdened Virtues: Virtue Ethics for Liberatory Struggles
Lisa Tessman

On Female Body Experience: "Throwing Like a Girl" and Other Essays
Iris Marion Young

Visible Identities: Race, Gender, and the Self
Linda Martín Alcoff

Women and Citizenship
Edited by Marilyn Friedman

Women's Liberation and the Sublime: Feminism, Postmodernism, Environment
Bonnie Mann

Analyzing Oppression
Ann E. Cudd

Ecological Thinking: The Politics of Epistemic Location
Lorraine Code

Self-Transformations: Foucault, Ethics, and Normalized Bodies
Cressida J. Heyes

Family Bonds: Genealogies of Race and Gender
Ellen K. Feder

Moral Understandings: A Feminist Study in Ethics, Second Edition
Margaret Urban Walker

The Moral Skeptic
Anita M. Superson

"You've Changed": Sex Reassignment and Personal Identity
Edited by Laurie J. Shrage

Dancing with Iris: The Philosophy of Iris Marion Young
Edited by Ann Ferguson and Mechthild Nagel

Philosophy of Science after Feminism
Janet A. Kourany

Philosophy of Science
after Feminism

Janet A. Kourany

OXFORD
UNIVERSITY PRESS

2010

OXFORD
UNIVERSITY PRESS

Oxford University Press, Inc., publishes works that further
Oxford University's objective of excellence
in research, scholarship, and education.

Oxford   New York
Auckland   Cape Town   Dar es Salaam   Hong Kong   Karachi
Kuala Lumpur   Madrid   Melbourne   Mexico City   Nairobi
New Delhi   Shanghai   Taipei   Toronto

With offices in
Argentina   Austria   Brazil   Chile   Czech Republic   France   Greece
Guatemala   Hungary   Italy   Japan   Poland   Portugal   Singapore
South Korea   Switzerland   Thailand   Turkey   Ukraine   Vietnam

Published by Oxford University Press, Inc.
198 Madison Avenue, New York, New York 10016

www.oup.com

Oxford is a registered trademark of Oxford University Press.

Library of Congress Cataloging-in-Publication Data
Kourany, Janet A.
Philosophy of science after feminism / Janet A. Kourany.
    p. cm. — (Studies in feminist philosophy)
Includes bibliographical references.
ISBN 978-0-19-973262-3; 978-0-19-973261-6 (pbk.)
1. Feminism and science. 2. Women in science. 3. Science—Philosophy. I. Title.
Q130.K684   2010
501—dc22   2009025889

9 8 7 6 5 4 3 2 1

Printed in the United States of America
on acid-free paper

To Jim, who suffered through the writing of this book nearly as much as I did but did not have half the fun. With unending thanks.

Preface

The goal of *Philosophy of Science after Feminism* is to provide the blueprint for a philosophy of science more socially engaged and socially responsible than the philosophy of science we have now, a philosophy of science that can help to promote a science more socially engaged and socially responsible than the science we have now. Feminists—feminist scientists and historians of science, as well as feminist philosophers of science—have already been pursuing this kind of philosophy of science in gender-related areas for three decades now. The strategy I adopt is to develop from their work a comprehensive new program of research for philosophy of science. How do I do this?

Chapter 1 introduces the kinds of normative questions regarding science feminists have been pursuing. These questions locate science within its wider societal context, investigating science's epistemic aspects as they are entangled with science's ethical, sociopolitical, and economic aspects. These questions are contrasted with the normative questions regarding science that mainstream philosophy of science currently pursues, the questions that investigate science's epistemic aspects in isolation from science's societal context.

Chapter 2 explores the twentieth-century roots of contemporary philosophy of science and its penchant for dealing with science as if science existed in a social/political/economic vacuum. It uncovers no defensible reasons, epistemic or otherwise, to indulge this penchant and many reasons not to. It also uncovers, in the early-twentieth-century work of the Vienna Circle, an important historical precedent for doing philosophy of science in a more socially connected way. A contemporary program for a "contextualized" philosophy of science inspired by the work of feminists might therefore be an attractive option.

Chapter 3 thus takes up the feminists' normative questions regarding science introduced in chapter 1 together with the various feminist science studies approaches they have engendered: the methodological approach rationalized by the ideal of value-free science, the social approach rationalized by the social-value-management ideal of science, and the naturalist approaches rationalized by the empiricist ideal of science. In the end, however, a new approach is found necessary: a political approach rationalized by the ideal of socially responsible science. According to this approach, sound social values, as well as sound epistemic values, must control every aspect of the scientific research process, from the choice of research questions to the communication and application of results, this to be enforced by such political means as funding requirements on research.

Chapter 4 takes this approach beyond the gender contexts of chapters 1 and 3 and defends it against five important challenges: an epistemological challenge, an historical challenge, a sociological challenge, an economic challenge, and a political challenge.

Finally, chapter 5 deals with the fundamental issues that must be settled in order to apply this approach to all of science. The upshot is a research program for philosophy of science geared to the development of a new, more comprehensive understanding of scientific rationality, one that integrates the ethical with the epistemic, and the parallel development of a new, more socially valuable role for philosophers of science, that of public intellectuals.

Every author has a favorite place to write, a place where ideas seem to flow more easily or with greater warrant than they do in other places. My favorite place is the Zentrum für Interdisziplinäre Forschung (ZIF) at Bielefeld University in Germany. Parts of chapters 3 and 4 were written during the spring 2007 term while I was a fellow in the research group "Science in the Context of Application," and part of chapter 5 was written while I was a TransCoop resident fellow during June and July 2008. Chapter 4, in particular, would have been impossible without the weekly discussions and monthly workshops of the research group organized by Martin Carrier (Bielefeld University) and Alfred Nordmann (Technische Universität Darmstadt and University of South Carolina). Martin Carrier, Hans Glimell (University of Göteborg), and Torsten Wilholt (Bielefeld University), fellow members of the research group, were especially helpful. The University of Pittsburgh's Center for Philosophy of Science furnished another happy environment for writing parts of this book (in particular, parts of chapters 1 and 2 and a forerunner of chapter 3) in the spring term of 2004, when I was a visiting fellow there. I am grateful to the University of Notre Dame as well as Bielefeld's ZIF and Pittsburgh's Center for Philosophy of Science for research support during these times.

Every author also has a favorite person with whom to discuss her work, a person on whom she can try out ideas even at their earliest stages, when they are most in need of gentle treatment. My favorite person has been my partner, Jim Sterba. He has patiently and lovingly read the entire manuscript and given much shrewd advice. To him I dedicate this book. Our daughter, Sonya Kourany Sterba, now a budding quantitative psychologist, has also given freely of her time and insights. Whatever errors remain are mine alone.

Parts of what follows are based on previously published work. Some of the material in chapter 1 is drawn from "A Philosophy of Science for the

Twenty-First Century," *Philosophy of Science* 70, no. 1 (2003): 1–14;
and from "A Feminist Primer for Philosophers of Science," in Christian
Nimtz and Ansgar Beckermann, eds., *Philosophie und/als Wissenschaft*
(Paderborn: Mentis, 2005), 287–305. The last part of chapter 2 is based
on "Getting Philosophy of Science Socially Connected," *Philosophy of Science* 73, no. 5 (2006): 991–1002. Chapter 3 is a revised and expanded
version of "Replacing the Ideal of Value-Free Science," in Martin Carrier,
Don Howard, and Janet Kourany, eds., *The Challenge of the Social and the
Pressure of Practice: Science and Values Revisited* (Pittsburgh: University of
Pittsburgh Press, 2008), 87–111. And parts of chapter 5 draw on material
from "Philosophy of Science: A Subject with a Great Future," *Philosophy
of Science* 75, no. 5 (2008): 767–778. I am grateful to the Philosophy of
Science Association, Mentis Publishers, the University of Chicago Press,
and the University of Pittsburgh Press for permission to use this material.
I am grateful also to Peter Ohlin, philosophy editor at Oxford University
Press, and Cheshire Calhoun, series editor of Oxford's Studies in Feminist
Philosophy, for their sustained interest and support of this project.

Contents

Philosophy of Science
after Feminism

1

A Feminist Primer for Philosophers of Science

- Women worldwide work more than men but earn less and have less job security, less job quality, fewer benefits, fewer assets, less control over family resources, and less control over household decision making. Even when they work full-time for pay outside the home, "the available evidence shows that, across regions, women's nominal wages are roughly 20% lower than men's" (UNICEF 2006)—in the United States in 2007, the figure was 78 cents for every dollar that men earned (National Women's Law Center 2009). At the same time, women still do the majority of housework, child care, and elder care (UNICEF 2006).
- In many countries there is a greater preference for male children than for female children. In China, South Korea, India, Pakistan, Bangladesh, Nepal, Egypt, Syria, Haiti, Colombia, Costa Rica, and many other countries, female babies and female fetuses are killed because they are of the "wrong" sex. In China in 2005, between 120 and 130 males were born for every 100 females, and in India, the number of "vanished" females has now reached 700,000. In addition, male children frequently receive better nutrition, health care, and support than female children. All of this prenatal and postnatal son selection is likely to have severe social consequences in coming years and may even produce a surge in sexual violence and trafficking of women (UN News Centre 2007; UN News Service 2008).
- "Violence against women and girls continues unabated in every continent, country and culture" and "is a problem of pandemic proportions. At least one out of every three women around the world has been beaten, coerced into sex, or otherwise abused in her lifetime" (UNIFEM 2007). What's more, "women are at greatest risk of violence from men they know. In Australia, Canada, Israel, South Africa and the United States, 40–70% of female murder victims were killed by their partners" (UNFPA 2005).

- While rape is an ever-present fear of women worldwide, most
  of the world's rape laws conceive of rape as an offense against
  men—either the fathers of unmarried women or the husbands of
  married ones. Similarly, in war, rape is regularly used by one side's
  soldiers as the ultimate humiliation and punishment of the men on
  the other side. "Violence against women during or after armed
  conflicts has been reported in every international or non-international
  war-zone, including Afghanistan, Burundi, Chad, Colombia, Cote
  d'Ivoire, Democratic Republic of the Congo, Liberia, Peru, Rwanda,
  Sierra Leone, Chechnya/Russian Federation, Darfur, Sudan, northern
  Uganda and the former Yugoslavia" (UNICEF 2006). In Rwanda, up to half
  a million women were raped during the 1994 genocide, up to 60,000
  women were raped in the war in Croatia and Bosnia-Herzegovina, more
  than 32,000 cases of rape and sexual violence occurred between 2005
  and 2006 in the Democratic Republic of Congo's South Kivu
  province alone, and so on (UNICEF 2006).

THE ROLE OF SCIENCE

After "three waves" of feminist activism in the United States and centuries
of feminist thought and activism around the world, women are still not
the social equals of men. The above items only begin to tell the story.
Prostitution and pornography and the trafficking of women, female geni-
tal mutilation and honor killings, restrictions related to reproduction and
gender socialization and sexual harassment, and more problems still need
to be added to the above items to give a complete understanding of wom-
en's situation. Even so, the above items manage to convey some of the
central problems women confront: that women the world over are thought
inferior to men and, hence, deserving of inferior jobs, inferior wages, and
inferior treatment both in the home and outside it.

Science can be a powerful ally in the struggle for equality for women.
Science, after all, can expose society's prejudice against women for what
it is, and science can both justify the replacement of this prejudice with a
more adequate perspective and move society to accept the replacement.
All too frequently, however, science has done more to perpetuate and add
to the problems women confront than to solve them. For example, one of
psychology's central messages, historically, has been that women are inferior to men—intellectually, socially, sexually, and even morally (Marecek
1995; Wilkinson 1997). And biology historically has set for itself the task
of explaining the basis and origin of this inferiority in terms of what is
largely unchangeable—biology. This has had the effect of justifying—and,
thus, helping to perpetuate—women's inferior educational and employment opportunities, as well as women's inferior positions in the family,
government, and other social institutions.

Consider women's intellectual capacity, for example. For centuries it was claimed that women are intellectually inferior to men, and for centuries the basis for such inferiority was sought in biology. In the seventeenth century, women's brains were claimed to be too "cold" and "soft" to sustain rigorous thought. In the late eighteenth century, the female cranial cavity was claimed to be too small to hold a powerful brain. In the late nineteenth century, the exercise of women's brains was claimed to be damaging to women's reproductive health—was claimed, in fact, to shrivel women's ovaries. In the twentieth century, the lesser "lateralization" (hemispheric specialization) of women's brains compared with men's was claimed to make women inferior in visuospatial skills (including mathematical skills) (Schiebinger 1989; Fausto-Sterling 1992, 2000). And now, in the beginning of the twenty-first century, the claims continue: that women's brains are smaller than men's brains, even correcting for differences of body mass; that women's brains have less white matter (axonal material); that women's brains have less focused cortical activity (lower "neural efficiency"); that women's brains have lower cortical processing speed (lower conduction velocity in their white matter's axons); and so on. And once again, these differences are being linked to differences in intellectual capacity: that people with smaller brains have lower IQ test scores; that less focused cortical activity is associated with lower intellectual performance; that lower cortical processing speed is associated with lower working-memory performance, which is correlated with lower "fluid intelligence" scores; and so on (see Hamilton 2008 for an up-to-date account). At the same time, much attention now focuses on the mappings of brain activity produced by brain imaging, particularly fMRIs (functional magnetic resonance imaging), and the differences in "emotional intelligence" these disclose. But once again, the "male brain," the "systemizer" brain, comes out on top—is the more scientific brain, the more innovative brain, the more leadership-oriented brain, the more potentially "elite" brain, than the "female brain," the "empathizer" brain (Karafyllis and Ulshofer 2008). And the biological research continues.

And so does the psychological research—the research whose results the biological research is intended to explain. Indeed, by one estimate more than 15,000 "human cognitive sex difference" studies were done between 1968 and 2008, more than 4,000 of them between 1998 and 2008 alone.[1] Of course, there are problems with many of these studies: they fail to report findings of no sex differences (nonsignificant findings), they fail to report the effect size of sex differences they do find, they fail to include replication samples to back up their initial findings, they assume a biological basis in the absence of biological data or cross-cultural data, and so on (Halpern 2000). No matter. Sweeping conclusions regarding cognitive sex

---

1. This estimate results from running a search on JSTOR of studies using the combination of words "human cognitive sex differences" on August 20, 2008. The exact numbers were 15,032 studies done between 1968 and 2008 and 4,038 between 1998 and 2008.

differences are drawn nonetheless. For example, one leading researcher in
the field, Doreen Kimura, after reviewing this terrain of cognitive sex
difference research, reports that

> we can say with certainty that there are substantial stable sex differences in
> cognitive functions like spatial rotation ability [favoring males], mathematical
> reasoning [favoring males], and verbal memory [favoring females]; and in
> motor skills requiring accurate targeting [favoring males] and finger dexterity
> [favoring females]. We can also state with certainty that most of these sexually
> differentiated functions are strongly influenced by early and/or current hormo-
> nal environments [ultimately linked to genetic and evolutionary factors].
> (Kimura 2000b, 181; see also Kimura 2002b, 2004a)

The upshot: "It may turn out that the most objective, most appropriate
and fairest criteria for admission to a program or an occupation will favor
men in some cases and women in others. This in fact is to be expected if
the ability differences described in this book are as stable as most seem to
be" (Kimura 2000b, 185). As a result, Kimura suggests, we ought not to be
troubled by the current marked inequalities in participation and success
of women and men in, for example, mathematics, science, and engineering, and we certainly ought not to try to change the situation by, for
example, instituting or continuing scholarships or research awards earmarked
specifically for talented women (see, in this connection, Kimura 2000a,
2001, 2002a, 2004b, and 2006; and compare Pinker 2002 and 2005, and half
the authors in Ceci and Williams 2007). Of course, other leading researchers
contest these conclusions (see, e.g., Hyde 2000, Hines 2001, the other half
of the authors in Ceci and Williams 2007, and Ceci and Williams 2010).
Some of these researchers even raise questions about the motivation of
such research. For example, Jeremy Caplan and Paula Caplan suggest that
"studying 'sex differences' in cognition is not a neutral activity, any more
than studying 'racial differences' in cognition. As long as our society is
sexist, racist, or biased in any other way, any claim to find group differences is likely, sooner or later, to be held up as proof of the more powerful
group's superiority" (Caplan and Caplan 2005, 25). Janet Shibley Hyde is
more emphatic:

> Why gender? That is, why should the spotlight be on gender differences, rather
> than on a myriad of other possibilities, such as social class differences or eye-
> color differences? A major implication of the small effect size for gender differ-
> ences in mathematics performance is that within-gender differences are far
> greater than between-gender differences. Surely there are other dimensions of
> individual differences in mathematics performance (such as, perhaps, learning
> style) that would be far more productive for scientific research. (Hyde 2000)

Steven Rose is more emphatic still:

> If attempts to answer these group-difference questions are fraught with scien-
> tific fallacies, might there nonetheless be some public-policy implications
> making investigation worthwhile? The answer sometimes advanced is that if

there were such differences, and their causes were understood, the less well-endowed groups could be 'compensated' by some form of differentiated education. But in practice, claims that there are differences in intelligence between blacks and whites, or men and women, have always been used to justify a social hierarchy in which white males continue to occupy the premier positions (whether in the economy in general or natural science in particular). . . .

In a society in which racism and sexism were absent, the questions of whether whites or men are more or less intelligent than blacks or women would not merely be meaningless—they would not even be asked. (Rose 2009, 788)

Nevertheless, the research still continues.

But fields such as psychology and biology are not the only sources of the view that women are inferior to men—demonstrably inferior, scientifically. The historical sciences, too, have supported this view of women's inferiority through their modes of representation of the past, modes of representation marked by heroic exploits and spectacular accomplishments of men counterposed with lackluster doings and nonaccomplishments, if not complete invisibility, of women. Consider archaeology, for example, a field in which, traditionally, the search for origins and pivotal developments in human evolution defines the "big" questions. It is this search, in fact, that allows archaeologists to structure their discipline and make their sometime-stirring statements about human nature and human society when presenting the results of their research. Until very recently, however, what archaeologists have recognized as the "hallmarks" of human evolution—tools, fire, hunting, food storage, language, agriculture, metallurgy—have all been associated with men. Take agriculture. Although women have been firmly associated by archaeologists with plants, both with gathering them (before the emergence of agriculture) and with cultivating them (after), when archaeologists have turned to the profoundly culture-transforming shift in subsistence practice represented by the invention of agriculture, women have disappeared from discussion. Until the 1990s, for example, dominant explanations of the emergence of agriculture in the eastern woodlands of North America have posited either male shamans and their ceremonial use of gourd rattles as the catalysts for this transition or plants' "automatic" processes of adaptation to the environmentally disturbed areas of human living sites (in which case, the plants essentially domesticated themselves). According to these explanations, in short, either men invented agriculture, or no one did (Watson and Kennedy 1991). "We have had, it seems, little problem in attributing a great deal of the archaeological record to men (the more salient stone tools, the hunting of big game, the making of 'art,' the development of power politics, the building of pyramids and mounds, the invention of writing by priests or temple accountants, domesticating gourds in order to have them available for shamans' rattles, etc.)" (Conkey 2008, 49). In addition, archaeologists have had little problem leaving out of the archaeological record what might easily, even stereotypically, have involved the experiences and contributions of women, such as midwifery and mothering practices, the socialization and gendering of children, sexual activities and relationships, the development of pottery, the invention and use of tools in activities other than big-game hunting (e.g., in food preparation, leatherworking, grain harvesting, and woodworking), and the social negotiations surrounding death, burial, and inheritance, topics that also hold enormous importance for the evolution of humans (see, for the beginnings of change on such topics, Meskell 1998; Joyce 2000; Schmidt and Voss 2000; Wilkie 2003; Baxter 2005). As a result of this mode of representation of the past, this persistent association of men with the great turning points of human evolution, man as active, instrumental (as in man the toolmaker), man as provider, man as innovator, man as quintessentially human have been made to seem natural, inevitable. At the same time, woman as outside the domain of innovation and control, woman as not active (that is, passive) and less than quintessentially human have been made to seem natural and inevitable as well, and thus capable of explaining (and justifying) the gender inequalities we still find today (Conkey and Williams 1991; and see Conkey 2008).

Other scientific fields have perpetuated or added to the problems women confront, but in different ways than by documenting women's inferiority. Neglecting women's needs and priorities in economic model building, for example, has had dire effects on public policy relating to women. And neglecting women in both basic and clinical research—in, for example, heart disease, AIDS, and cancer research—has had dire effects on women's health care.

Start with economics (see, for what follows, Waring 1992, 1997; Ferber and Nelson 1993, 2003; Nelson 1996a, 1996b; Estin 2005). The central concept in current mainstream economics ("neoclassical" economics) is that of "the market," a place where rational, autonomous, self-interested agents with stable preferences interact for the purposes of exchange. These agents may be individual persons or collectives of various kinds, such as corporations, labor unions, and governments. The agents, in either case, exchange goods or services, with money facilitating the transactions, and the tool of choice for analyzing these transactions is mathematics. Indeed, high status is assigned in economics to formal mathematical models of rational choice. What tends to remain invisible, however, or inadequately treated, is women.

Take women's experiences in the family. Since the focus in mainstream economics is on the "public" realm (industry and government), "private" collectives such as the family tend to get scant attention. And since the prototype for economic agents is individual persons, and masculine persons at that,[2] when families *are* attended to, they are most commonly

2. That is, the rational, autonomous, self-interested persons that men are supposed to be by the norms of masculinity, rather than the emotional, social, other-directed persons that women are supposed to be by the norms of femininity.

treated as if they were individuals themselves, with all their internal workings a "black box." Or they are treated as if they had a dominant "head" who makes all the decisions in accordance with "his" own (perhaps altruistic) preferences. Either way of treating the family, of course, leaves women invisible as agents in their own right in the family. More recently, however, families have been treated by some economists as (cooperative or noncooperative) collective decision-making partnerships. But since, here as elsewhere in mainstream economics, the focus is on simplified mathematical models portraying the interactions of rational, autonomous agents, these collective decision-making partnerships end by being models of marital *couples*. Children, not yet fully rational, certainly not autonomous, and threatening to the tractability of the models, are either conceptualized as "consumption goods" or not conceptualized at all. Left invisible, therefore, are women in the family as caregivers, as agents who historically[3] have borne the bulk of the responsibility for the nurturing and education of children and the care of the sick and elderly. The upshot is that women's needs and priorities in families are left invisible and, with them, the impact on women and their charges of public policies:

> Any model of the effect of price changes, or taxes or transfers on family behavior must, implicitly or explicitly, rely on a theory of how families function. Beyond the social scientists' need to understand, lies the policy-makers' need to make wise policies. Better knowledge about what is happening in the family could improve policies related to child poverty and child support, household-sector savings rates, welfare and job training, the tax treatment of dependents and family-related expenses, social security, elder care, healthcare, and inheritance taxation, to name a few areas. (Nelson 1996a, 60)

Mainstream economics obscures women's situation in families in other ways as well. Indeed, it essentially offers only one theory of why the household is organized the way it is. According to this theory,

> individuals decide whether to marry, have children, or divorce based on a comparison of the direct and indirect benefits and costs of different actions. It conceives of people in family relations as rational, utility-maximizing actors, facing a range of choices with limited supplies of time, energy, wealth, and other resources. It imagines that for most goods there are substitutes, although recognizing that these may not be perfect, and postulates that individual actors have an ability to choose freely. (Estin 2005, 434–435)

Finally, this theory describes the gender-based division of labor in households as "efficient" insofar as that division of labor allows a family to generate a maximum level of utility with a given set of resources—describes it as efficient even though that division of labor often results from factors such as discrimination against women in the workplace, often involves wives bearing much heavier loads of work and family responsibilities than

---

3. "Tradition, in particular, may be a far more powerful force in determining the allocation of household tasks than rational optimization" (Ferber and Nelson 1993, 6).

their husbands, and often leaves wives vulnerable to domestic abuse and other effects of lower status in marriage and financial problems with divorce. Wedded to efficiency as a normative ideal, however, this theory does not invite exploration of policies aimed at restructuring the traditional household and how such policies might impact other problem areas for women, such as the gender wage gap. As a result, mainstream economic theory, with its focus on economic efficiency, serves to reinforce and justify a social order systematically harmful to women.

Medical research has also perpetuated or added to, rather than ameliorated, the problems women confront (see, for what follows, Rosser 1994; Weisman and Cassard 1994; Gura 1995; Mann 1995; Meinert 1995; Sherman, Temple, and Merkatz 1995; Schiebinger 1999). Until 1993—when Congress passed the National Institutes of Health Revitalization Act that mandated the inclusion of women and minorities in U.S. medical research—females tended to be neglected in both basic and clinical research. Three of the more egregious areas of neglect were heart disease, AIDS, and breast-cancer research, despite the fact that heart disease is the leading cause of death among women, AIDS is increasing more rapidly among women than among the members of any other group, and breast cancer has for years been the most frequently occurring cancer in women. The result was that these diseases were often not detected in women—often not even suspected—and not properly managed when they were detected.

Consider just heart disease. Slightly more than one out of every two women in the United States will die from cardiovascular illnesses. Yet until the 1990s, heart disease was defined as a male disease and studied primarily in white, middle-aged, middle-class males. The large, well-publicized, well-funded studies of the past are illustrative: the Physicians' Health Study, whose results were published in 1989, examined the effect of low-dose aspirin therapy on the risk of heart attack in 22,071 male physicians; the Multiple Risk Factor Intervention Trial (MR. FIT), whose results were published in 1990, examined the impact of losing weight, giving up smoking, and lowering cholesterol levels on the risk of heart attack in 12,866 men; the Health Professionals Follow-Up Study, whose results were also published in 1990, examined the relationship between coffee consumption and heart disease in 45,589 men. And these studies were no exceptions. In a 1992 *Journal of the American Medical Association* analysis of all clinical trials of medications used to treat acute heart attack published in English-language journals between 1960 and 1991, for example, it was found that fewer than 20 percent of the subjects were women. "When I began studying cardiovascular disease, it was all about women taking care of their husbands' hearts," recalls cardiologist Bernadine Healy, who, as the first female director of the National Institutes of Health from 1991 to 1993, did much to change the situation. "Heart disease in women was either trivialized or ignored for years" (quoted in Gura 1995, 771).

The consequences of that neglect of women were far from trivial, however. Since women were not researched along with the men, it was not discovered for years that women differed from men in symptoms, patterns of disease development, and reactions to treatment. As a result, heart disease in women was often not detected, and it was often not even suspected. What's more, it was not properly managed when it was detected. Drug treatments were a particularly glaring example. Drugs that were beneficial to many men caused problems in many women. For example, some clot-dissolving drugs used to treat heart attacks in men caused bleeding problems in women, and some standard drugs used to treat high blood pressure tended to lower men's mortality from heart attack while they raised women's mortality. What's more, the dosage of drugs commonly prescribed for men was often not suitable for women. Some drugs (such as antidepressants) varied in their effects over the course of the menstrual cycle, while others (such as acetaminophen, an ingredient in many pain relievers) were eliminated in women at slower rates than in men. Studying only, or primarily, men resulted in failures to prescribe appropriate kinds and doses of drugs for women, as well as, of course, failures to offer other treatments (cardiac catheterization, coronary angioplasty, angiography, artery bypass surgery) at appropriate times. And it resulted in women's limited access to experimental therapies.

Of course, since 1993 the medical-research agenda has become more inclusive. Nonetheless, the effects of the old exclusions still linger. For example, women consume roughly 80% of the pharmaceuticals used in the United States, but they are still frequently prescribed drugs and dosages devised for men's conditions and average weights and metabolisms. As a result, adverse reactions to drugs occur twice as often in women as in men. "The net effect of gender bias in medical research and education is that women suffer unnecessarily and die. . . . Not only are drugs developed for men potentially dangerous for women; drugs potentially beneficial to women may [have been] eliminated in early testing because the test group [did] not include women" (Schiebinger 1999, 115).

Science, in short, has done much to perpetuate and add to the problems women confront rather than solve them. But, of course, science has also produced much of the available information regarding these problems, and scientists have also provided at least some of the wherewithal for solving them. Psychologists, for example, have explored at least some of women's "inferiority"—women's lack of assertiveness, low self-esteem, and poor self-confidence, and women's (and men's) underestimation and undervaluation of women's achievements and potential—and have explained this inferiority in terms of prevailing "gender schemas"; and anthropologists have provided abundant evidence to show that such inferiority is not universal. Psychologists have also devised "compensatory socialization" type therapy and various self-help and group-change type programs, as well as "public health" type approaches (e.g., for domestic violence), in response (di Leonardo 1992; Marecek 1995; Stefan 1996;

Wilkinson 1997; Valian 1998, 2005). Anthropologists have researched "rape-prone" and "rape-free" cultures and, based on this research, have made recommendations for change, especially on college campuses (Sanday 1981, 1990, 1996). Economists have studied the effects of current economic restructuring on women—for example, the expansion of jobs with greater flexibility but lower wages and fewer opportunities for advancement, and growing inequalities in employment experience among women of different racial/ethnic and class groups. And they have explored the benefits of implementing comparable-worth and other policies as strategies to address some of the worst of these effects (see, e.g., the essays in Mutari, Boushey, and Fraher 1997, especially the essay by Mutari and Figart and the essay by Figart and Lapidus, as well as the essays in Ferber and Nelson 2003, especially the essay by Beneria). The examples could go on and on. But a large part of this work has been done by feminist scientists on the margins of their fields. This again shows that science can be a powerful ally in the struggle for equality for women but all too frequently has not been.

TOWARD A NEW ROLE FOR SCIENCE

Can anything be done to change this situation? *Should* anything be done to change this situation? Consider, to begin with, the questions that are pursued in science. Should research of interest and benefit to women be prioritized (e.g., through funding initiatives for government-funded science, tax incentives for industry-funded science, and conditions on the tax-exempt status of foundation-funded science) so that scientists are encouraged to pursue such research, while research that neglects women's interests and needs is deprioritized or even prohibited?[4] More radically, should research be similarly prioritized that promises support for egalitarian views and programs (e.g., research that seeks to explain different levels of success between men and women on the basis of social factors)? In this way, again, scientists would be encouraged to pursue such research. At the same time, should research be *deprioritized* that *threatens* egalitarian views and programs (e.g., research that seeks to explain different levels of male/female success on the basis of biological differences)? And what about the results of research? Should special provisions be instituted here, too, in order to produce a science more helpful to women? For example, should ways of evaluating research be adopted that favor egalitarian views—such as requiring higher standards of evidence for inegalitarian

4. Neglecting women's interests and needs means, for example, excluding women from or underrepresenting women in clinical studies in medical research when the studies relate to non-gender-specific conditions such as heart disease. It also means, for example, failing to conduct sufficient research on serious conditions that primarily or exclusively concern women, such as breast cancer.

views or requiring the acceptance of egalitarian (or more egalitarian) views whenever empirically possible (e.g., in those cases of underdetermination in which practical action needs to be taken)?

Or would the above possibilities jeopardize science as an impartial search for truth, *all* truth? And isn't it just this aspect of science that can enable science to be a powerful ally in the fight for equality for women—since the fight is against prejudice and ignorance and misinformation about women, all the things that scientists as impartial seekers and exposers of truth can combat? Shouldn't scientists and policy makers, therefore, be left free to make decisions regarding the pursuit and evaluation of research on purely scientific grounds, purely "epistemic" grounds, rather than on social grounds?

Then again, isn't such epistemic "freedom" just what we have had, just what has produced not science as an ally in the fight for equality for women but science as a perpetuator of inequality? But perhaps this is because science has been dominated by men, men who have been raised in sexist and androcentric societies and trained within sexist and androcentric scientific traditions, men who, moreover, profit from this sexism and androcentrism. Perhaps, then, what should be done, so that science can be an ally in the fight for equality for women, is to institute some kind of robust affirmative-action policy for women in science, one that will ensure not only that women join the scientific community but also that they stay there and flourish and become integrated into every area and every level of that enterprise. Or perhaps what should be done is to expose scientists to feminist perspectives throughout their training and strive to build such perspectives into their standard methodological procedures in order to screen out gender bias. Or perhaps what should be done is to rely not on feminist perspectives imported into science but on the diverse feminist perspectives of scientists themselves, in confrontation with the diverse nonfeminist and antifeminist perspectives of other scientists. That is to say, perhaps what should be done is to institute a robust affirmative-action policy for diversity in science, one that will ensure that scientists are drawn from all segments of society—from all political groups, all races, all classes, all sexual orientations, and so on. In this way all perspectives, including all manner of feminist perspectives, will be represented, and all perspectives will be critiqued. But what values will form the basis of such critiques, the traditional ones of our traditional sexist and androcentric science or new ones, and, if the latter, what new ones?

Then again, perhaps what should be done is nothing at all. After all, *why should* science be an ally in the struggle for equality for women? One reason, of course, is that science has already done so much to add to and perpetuate women's inequality and promises to do still more. Hence, some rectification is in order. Another reason is that society—both women and men—ultimately pays for science, through taxes and through consumer spending. And society is deeply affected by science: science shapes our lives and, perhaps most important, science shapes our conception of ourselves. As A. J. Heschel explained almost a half-century ago: "A theory about the stars never becomes a part of the being of the stars. A theory about man enters his consciousness, determines his self-understanding, and modifies his very existence. The image of a man affects the nature of man. . . . We become what we think of ourselves" (Heschel 1965, 7). Another reason, in short, is that science, so much a shaper of society and so much a beneficiary of society, should be deeply responsive to the needs of society. But surely one of the needs of society—of both women and men—is justice, and equality for women is one aspect of that justice. There are, then, two reasons for thinking that science should be an ally in the struggle for equality for women. How telling are these reasons, and are there others as well? And what countervailing reasons might there be?

TOWARD A NEW ROLE FOR PHILOSOPHY OF SCIENCE

The questions of the above section cry out for attention, since they directly concern the well-being of half the population. Indeed, they directly concern the well-being of a good many more of the population than that. For the above questions have analogues that pertain to race and ethnicity, sexual orientation, physical ability and disability, and other struggles for social justice. Science can be a powerful ally in these struggles, too, and in these struggles, too, science has all too frequently done more for the cause of inequality than for equality. Call the above questions and their analogues, therefore, questions regarding the social responsibility of science, or SRS questions for short. These are the questions feminist scientists and philosophers and historians of science have been wrestling with for well over three decades now, and their answers have been varied. What relation does their enterprise have to mainstream philosophy of science?

Certainly, SRS questions are concerned with normative issues surrounding science—very much a standard philosophy of science undertaking and that which typically distinguishes it from the various social studies of science—and certainly SRS questions are concerned with these normative issues in the context of actual science, a sine qua non of philosophy of science since its "naturalistic turn." The normative issues with which SRS questions are concerned, moreover, relate to standard philosophy of science fare—to research pursuit and evaluation and the ultimate goals of science, for example; to what makes for scientific objectivity and what threatens it; to the relation between the epistemic and the social.

The normative issues with which SRS questions are concerned, however, also differ from standard philosophy of science fare. To begin with, they deal with the social effects of scientific knowledge—the beneficial effects that scientific knowledge *can have* on the struggles for equality of women (gays, African-Americans, etc.), as well as the unfortunate effects that scientific knowledge *has had* on these same struggles for equality.

Most contemporary philosophy of science, by contrast, deals with the knowledge that science produces, *period*—deals, that is, with science as a purely "epistemic" or "cognitive" enterprise. If anything social leaks into philosophers' reflections on science, it generally appears in their accounts of the goings-on within scientific laboratories and scientific conference rooms—the symbiosis of experimental and theoretical practices, for example, or the interplay between cooperation and competition, or the factors influencing consensus formation. The "social," for these philosophers, stops at the doors of scientists' immediate environments. It does not extend to such things as health care, or the labor market, or the educational establishment. The social effects of scientific knowledge, if considered at all, constitute separate questions that come after the epistemic ones. Philip Kitcher's perceptive and candid admissions in the final paragraphs of *The Advancement of Science* seem perfectly applicable to this work of most contemporary philosophers of science:

> The foregoing chapters leave untouched some of the largest questions about science. . . . To claim, as I have done, that the sciences achieve certain epistemic goals that we rightly prize is not enough—for the practice of science might be disadvantageous to human well-being in more direct, practical ways. A convincing account of practical progress will depend ultimately on articulating an ideal of human flourishing against which we can appraise various strategies for doing science. . . .
>
> We can envisage a very general problem of optimization. Given an ideal of human flourishing, how should we pursue our collective investigation of nature [or, he adds later, how should we modify the collective investigation we have now]? Beyond my attempt to understand the *epistemic* features of the scientific enterprise lies this far broader question about science, a question that a critical philosophy of science ought to address. (Kitcher 1993, 391)

SRS questions, in short, are examples of Kitcher's far larger, far broader questions about science, the questions that any "critical philosophy of science ought to address" but that most contemporary philosophy of science has not addressed. For SRS questions deal with the appraisal of "various strategies for doing science"—that is, various programs of research and evaluative criteria and ways of organizing scientific communities and the like—against an egalitarian "ideal of human flourishing," and SRS questions deal, as well, with the new strategies and modifications of existing strategies that such an appraisal might suggest. But this is not the only way in which SRS questions differ from most contemporary philosophy of science. SRS questions also treat the appraisal of science in terms of an egalitarian ideal of human flourishing as central. As we have seen, even modes of evaluation of research fall under its sway. (Remember what the SRS questions include: Should ways of evaluating research be adopted that favor egalitarian views—such as requiring higher standards of evidence for inegalitarian views? Or should scientists be exposed to feminist perspectives throughout their training, and should such perspectives be built into their standard methodological procedures, in order to screen out gender bias? And so on.) In *The Advancement of Science*, by contrast, Kitcher treats his far larger, far broader questions regarding the appraisal of science in terms of human flourishing as an *addition* to the epistemic questions that have been his main concern, as almost an afterthought to them (his far larger, far broader questions, after all, occupy the very last page of a nearly 400-page book). Even Kitcher's groundbreaking *Science, Truth, and Democracy* (2001), quite exceptional in contemporary philosophy of science for focusing serious attention on these far larger, far broader questions, still ends up segregating the strategies of scientific evaluation from the social preferences that, Kitcher argues, should shape research priorities and applications (see Kitcher 2001, chapter 10).

There are other differences as well. Both SRS questions and contemporary philosophy of science deal with the epistemic features of science. But SRS questions also deal with the social conditions that encourage science to have the particular epistemic features that it does—for example, the funding priorities that lie behind scientific research or the modes of recruitment and training that shape scientific communities. These are the social conditions that, in most contemporary philosophy of science, have been branded part of the "context of discovery" and shunted out accordingly. Unlike most contemporary philosophy of science, moreover, SRS questions are motivated by the need and desire for social change and invite social/political/epistemic initiatives intended to bring about that change, such as the proposal of new funding programs for science, or new kinds of recruitment or training programs, or the support of new epistemic values. By ignoring the larger social context of science and its relations with the epistemic—indeed, by providing a picture of science that portrays it as detached from this larger social context—most contemporary philosophy of science, by contrast, helps to keep invisible those features of science that need revision, and how they need revision, in order to bring about desirable social change. Most contemporary philosophy of science thereby helps to perpetuate the status quo. Unlike most contemporary philosophy of science, in short, SRS questions encourage a comprehensive, well-integrated exploration of science in society and a comprehensive, well-integrated plan of action to bring about needed change in both science and society.

Contemporary mainstream philosophy of science, then, is quite different from the enterprise defined by SRS questions, which is to say that contemporary mainstream philosophers of science may not be especially well equipped, professionally, to deal with such questions. If SRS questions nonetheless cry out for attention, philosophers of science may have to transform their pedagogical, research, and other activities to respond. Why should they want to do this? As already stated, philosophy of science is distinguished from the various social studies of science by its normative concerns: it aims not only to describe science but to critically evaluate it as well. Contemporary philosophy of science, however, limits this critical role to a purely epistemic one, even though most philosophers of science are systematically trained in ethics and political philosophy as well as logic and epistemology. Pursuing SRS questions would allow philosophers of science to broaden this critical role to encompass social critique as well as epistemic critique and would allow them to thoroughly integrate these critiques. Pursuing SRS questions would thus provide philosophers of science with a richer, more socially valuable program of research, one with social/political as well as epistemological importance.

Should philosophers of science now be convinced? Hardly. Much more needs to be said.

PLAN OF THE BOOK

To begin with, if contemporary philosophy of science is quite different from the enterprise defined by SRS questions, perhaps there are good reasons for the difference, good reasons for philosophers of science to do what they have been doing, ignoring the social context of science and focusing purely on the epistemic. Perhaps there are good reasons for philosophers of science *as* philosophers of science *not* to get into the business of social action and social change. But if there are such good reasons, what are they? The roots of twentieth-century philosophy of science and the contemporary philosophy of science scene lie in the Vienna Circle, and recent scholarship reveals that the Vienna Circle was motivated not only by abstract logical and epistemological concerns but by concrete social and political ones as well. Indeed, for the members of the Vienna Circle science could, and ultimately would, reform society, and philosophy of science could, and ultimately would, expedite that reform. Why did philosophy of science change from this socially engaged program of research and practice to the socially disengaged program of Anglo-American logical empiricism, and how was the change accomplished? What's more, how was the social disengagement maintained through the twentieth-century philosophy of science that followed? Were good reasons for the lack of social engagement ever involved? These will be the questions explored in chapter 2.

But even if good reasons were never involved—good reasons for ignoring the social context of science and focusing purely on the epistemic—what follows? Are there good reasons for philosophers of science to depart from their now long tradition of research and teaching? Pursuing SRS questions would provide philosophers of science with a richer, more socially valuable program of research, to be sure, one with social/political as well as epistemological importance. But at a cost. SRS questions, after all, raise a number of different kinds of social-value questions to which philosophers of science are largely unaccustomed. First, do social values belong in science at all, or should science be value-free, an impartial search for truth? Second, if social values do belong in science, which ones belong? Do they include, for example, egalitarian values, and which egalitarian values? Third, where do these social values belong in science? In the area of research pursuit and funding? In the area of research (theory, hypothesis, model, concept, data, method, etc.) evaluation? In the area of research team or research community organization or science pedagogy? In other areas? And fourth, what specific changes in science need to be made as a result? For example, should research of interest and benefit to women be prioritized in our national science policy? And so forth. Would pursuing SRS questions, therefore, be simply too laborious an undertaking for philosophers of science? Not at all. Feminists have already cleared the way. In chapter 3, some of the most important contributions of these feminists will be explored and the outlines of answers to SRS questions delineated.

Of course, all of this feminist work has been the subject of sometimes strident criticism. Feminist work, in fact, has been a central target in the so-called "Science Wars" debates. What criticisms in this literature relate to the answers to SRS questions sketched in chapter 3, and what other criticisms might prove worrisome as well—for example, criticisms based on historical cases (e.g., Soviet science or Nazi science) in which social values operated in science to the detriment of the science? How might these criticisms be responded to? This will be the focus of chapter 4.

If the outlines of defensible answers to SRS questions lie ready at hand by the outset of chapter 5, what is there left for philosophers of science to do? Why are SRS questions not a very limited project—one simply for feminists, and completed in the space of only one book at that—and hence of no particular interest to philosophers of science? And what is in the offing if philosophers of science actually pursue the project? With its emphasis on social values and social change and the changes in science these mandate, this new program for philosophy of science seems to catapult philosophers of science right out of academia into the political realm, working to bring about social change via the social/political/epistemic initiatives they defend. Will such a program for philosophy of science thereby compromise the integrity of philosophy of science as an academic discipline? These queries will form the terrain of chapter 5. Its landmarks will indicate not only the importance of the issues covered by SRS questions but also their range. Indeed, SRS questions concern not only the possibility of science's being an ally in the struggle for (gender, racial/ethnic, sexual orientation, etc.) equality but also the possibility of science's being an ally in the effort to create a sustainable environment, maintain peace among nations, and so on. In short, there is plenty left for philosophers of science to do. But will its doing compromise the integrity of philosophy of science? Why should it? After all, the new program for philosophy of science offered here is not, in this respect, so very different from other currently existing academic enterprises. Think of economics and political science, for example, whose practitioners often play at least advisory roles in governments here and abroad, in organizations such as Amnesty International, in labor unions, and in various civil-rights organizations, all without impairing their academic credentials. The new program for philosophy of science offered here is not even so very different from other currently existing academic enterprises in science studies. Consider the history of science, for example. Beginning in the 1950s, American historians of science have testified before U.S. congressional committees on the desirability of creating a Department of Science (A. Hunter Dupree), on the tension between democratic and elite science (Daniel Kevles), on ethics in science (June Goodfield and Dorothy Nelkin), on the general value of outside experts trained in the social sciences in the formulation of science policy (Alex Roland), and on many other issues related to national science policy. They have also provided information and policy advice to the National Aeronautics and Space Administration and the National Science Foundation, as well as private corporations. Reflecting on these activities and on current and future policy needs, historian of science John Heilbron has called for research and modes of disseminating the results of that research—from philosophers and sociologists of science, as well as historians—that "contribute to the formation of a balanced and humane national science policy" (Heilbron 1987, 563). The new program for philosophy of science offered here fits right in with this goal. And well it should. Few institutions today can do as much harm or as much good as science, and few institutions of science can do as much of either as the U.S. science establishment. It is high time philosophers joined with historians and sociologists of science in just the way Heilbron suggests to help steer science in the one direction and away from the other. The new program for philosophy of science offered in this book enables them to do just that. Such, at least, will be my message in chapter 5.

2

The Legacy of Twentieth-Century
Philosophy of Science

The transition to the twenty-first century has been met with many reflections and assessments of the goings-on of the twentieth—everything from the atomic bomb to the Beatles, women's studies to space exploration. If we turn our gaze on philosophy of science in the same way that critics have turned their gaze on these, what should we conclude? What kind of enterprise was philosophy of science in the twentieth century and, even more important, how successful was it?

THE PROFESSIONALIZATION OF PHILOSOPHY
OF SCIENCE

It was not until the middle of the twentieth century that philosophy of science came into its own as a professional discipline. By then, new academic departments and privately endowed centers had formed that were devoted exclusively to philosophy of science, new philosophy of science journals and conference series and book series were launched, and government support for research was expanding through such sources as the National Science Foundation. In addition, philosophy of science by then enjoyed increasing prestige within traditional philosophy departments and a preeminent place among the various science studies fields (for more details, see Howard 2003).

All of this prominence achieved by philosophy of science was doubtless connected, at least in part, to the distinctive goal philosophy of science had adopted. Unlike other areas of philosophy, such as ethics or epistemology or metaphysics, philosophy of science sought to engage with and contribute to *science*, then (and probably still) considered the most impressive, most progressive, most demanding of human endeavors. And unlike other science studies fields, such as history of science and sociology of science—which also engaged with science—philosophy of science sought not simply to describe science but to articulate and even improve upon what lay at the heart of its success, scientific rationality itself. What's more, philosophy of science had special resources for pursuing this goal, the then-developing field of formal logic and the rich tradition of empiricist epistemology. Hence the fashionable name for the enterprise: logical empiricism.

Hans Reichenbach had prepared the way for philosophy of science's distinctive goal with his famous distinction between the "context of discovery" and the "context of justification."[1] In his book *Experience and Prediction*, published the year he began teaching in the United States, 1938, Reichenbach had proclaimed that the task of the philosophy of science was to analyze the "internal structure" of scientific knowledge, not the "external relations" this knowledge enters into either with scientists or with society (see Reichenbach 1938, 3–8). That astronomers belong in general to the bourgeois class of society, he said, that they construct huge observatories containing telescopes in order to watch the stars—or, we might add, that the results of their star-gazing are used by the military, which therefore pays for the huge observatories—are of concern only to sociologists, not to philosophers. Of concern to philosophers, said Reichenbach, are only the "internal relations" between data from telescopes and theories about the stars. This internal structure of scientific knowledge of concern to philosophers, however, does not relate to the system of connections actually followed in the thinking of scientists. That, indeed, is the province of psychology. Instead, "what [philosophy of science] intends is to construct thinking processes in a way in which they ought to occur if they are to be ranged in a consistent system; or to construct justifiable sets of operations which can be intercalated between the starting-point and the issue of thought-processes, replacing the real intermediate links"—in much the same way scientists publicly present their findings in contrast to the way they come to discover them, but without the "many abbreviations and silently tolerated inexactitudes" and "traces of subjective motivation" that still mar even the best public presentations (5, 7). Philosophy of science "thus considers a logical substitute rather than real processes," "a better way of thinking than actual thinking," a *"rational reconstruction"* (5, 6).[2] Reichenbach introduced the terms *context of discovery* and *context of justification* to mark this important distinction between the way scientists actually come to produce scientific knowledge and philosophers' idealized rational reconstruction of that production process.

To the context of discovery, the province of such fields as the psychology and sociology and history of science, then, had been consigned everything "external" to scientific knowledge, everything social: the actual thought processes and interactions of scientists (both with one another and with nonscientists) that occur as scientists propose and investigate

1. The distinction was not original to Reichenbach, however. Ronald Giere points out that versions of it had been common in German philosophy for more than 50 years (Giere 1999, 13).

2. The term *rational reconstruction*, Reichenbach pointed out, derived from Rudolf Carnap.

and accept or reject hypotheses, the way these hypotheses and the questions that call them forth grow out of scientists' interests and values and cultural environments as well as their intellectual perspectives, and the social consequences of entertaining and accepting such hypotheses. To the context of justification, on the other hand, the province of philosophy of science, had been assigned only the logical, only the "epistemic." Of course, some of those external things (e.g., some of the actual thought processes of scientists), after they were rationally reconstructed, would become part of the context of justification, the province of philosophy of science. But when this happened, those external things would cease to be social at all, would become, in fact, logical fictions, "logical substitutes rather than real processes." True, the rational reconstructions would have to remain in correspondence with the actual thinking of scientists. That, indeed, was the "descriptive task" Reichenbach urged on philosophers of science. But the rational reconstructions also had to provide a rendition of that thinking that maximized its logical coherence and cogency—that was the "critical task" Reichenbach urged on philosophers of science.

By mid-century, then, following Reichenbach, philosophers of science had developed a taxonomy of the various kinds of knowledge claims scientists make—"empirical generalizations," "empirical laws," "theories," "explanations," "observation statements," and so on—and an analysis of each of these kinds of claims using the resources of formal logic and empiricist epistemology. All of this was to aid in the rational reconstruction of science. Thus, theories were analyzed as axiom systems partially interpreted by an observational language itself interpreted on the basis of observation. Explanations invoking such theories were analyzed as the logical derivation of the statements to be explained (the "explananda") from the theories and statements of initial conditions (the "explanans"). Scientific laws were analyzed as true spatiotemporally unrestricted statements of universal or statistical form, whose nonlogical terms were either observational (for empirical laws) or theoretical (for theoretical laws). The assessment of scientific (empirical or theoretical) hypotheses was analyzed as the logical derivation of observation statements ("predictions") from those hypotheses (in conjunction with statements of initial conditions) and the comparison of such predictions with statements describing the results of observation or experiment. Scientific progress was analyzed as the extension of scientific knowledge—for example, the addition of new empirical laws and theories to existing ones—as well as the greater systematization of existing knowledge—for example, the deductive subsumption (explanation) of scientific theories by more general theories and even whole disciplines by other disciplines. And so on. This taxonomy of the kinds of knowledge claims scientists make together with their analyses provided the framework within which Reichenbach's critical/descriptive program of rational reconstruction was to be carried out. The success of philosophy of science's ambitious venture must have seemed assured.

OBSTACLES TO SUCCESS

If the middle of the twentieth century was the time when philosophy of science came into its own as a professional discipline distinct from both science and the other areas of science studies and philosophy, it was also the time, ironically enough, when philosophy of science was least successful. True, philosophy of science by then exhibited breathtaking logical and epistemic virtuosity in the analyses it put forward. But it also lacked something absolutely central to its success: relevance to science. By the late 1950s and early 1960s, Thomas Kuhn, Paul Feyerabend, Norwood Russell Hanson, Stephen Toulmin, and many other distinguished philosophers and historians of science complained that philosophy of science simply failed to make contact with actual science. The problem was philosophy of science's exclusive concern with (Reichenbach's legacy!) the logic of science. Logic, of course, was relevant to scientific rationality, philosophy of science's overarching concern. But logic was far from the whole story.

Consider, for example, the issue of scientific justification—in particular, the justification of scientific theories. By mid-century, the "received view" of justification (see, e.g., Suppe 1974) was the hypothetico-deductive model of confirmation associated with the work of Rudolf Carnap and Carl Hempel. According to this view, scientific theories—such as Darwin's theory of natural selection or Newton's theory of mechanics—postulate entities and processes (such as evolution and gravitational attraction) that cannot be directly observed, in order to explain what can (e.g., fossil remains and planetary positions). As a result, theories cannot be directly tested by observation and experiment; they can only be indirectly tested by deducing from them consequences regarding observables and comparing those consequences with the results of observation and experiment. Because such theories are very general, however—they allow a potentially infinite number of observable consequences to be deduced—they can only be partially tested in this way. That is to say, they can only be partially justified or "confirmed" to different degrees if their observable consequences are verified, showing that they are, to a greater or lesser degree, probably true; they can never be completely justified or definitely shown to be true. More specifically, each verified observable consequence of a theory is a positive instance of the theory, adding to the degree of confirmation or degree of probability of the theory. And if a great many positive instances of a theory have been observed while no negative instances have been observed—of course, the instances should be as diversified as possible—then the degree of confirmation or degree of probability of the theory will be high. If, on the other hand, even a single negative instance of the theory is observed, then the theory will have been falsified. According to the "received view" of scientific justification current at mid-century, then, theory justification was nothing more than an inductive logical relation between a theory and its verified observable consequences.

The problem with this received view of justification, however, was that it did not take account of aspects of scientific appraisal widely thought to be significant. One such aspect was the prediction of novelty. Scientists and philosophers as diverse as Christopher Clavius, René Descartes, Gottfried Leibniz, Christiaan Huygens, William Whewell, Charles Sanders Peirce, and Pierre Duhem had argued for years that the prediction of surprising phenomena—phenomena that were either completely unknown or unexpected according to current conceptions or experimental results—counted more heavily in favor of a theory than the prediction of phenomena that were already known and perhaps even built into the theory right from the start; and by the middle of the twentieth century, these eminent scientists and philosophers were joined by others, such as Karl Popper and his followers (who, in fact, claimed that *only* novel predictions supported a theory). A frequently cited example concerned Augustin Fresnel, who won the French Academy of Sciences' Grand Prix in 1819 for his wave theory of diffraction even though the scientific establishment in general and the French Academy in particular were at that time dominated by particle theorists. Although the prize topic declared in 1817 was a mathematical theory to explain diffraction, and although Fresnel's mathematical theory agreed well with known experimental results, the committee evaluating it (made up largely of advocates of particle theories) was not fully convinced, and Simeon Denis Poisson, one of its members, devised a further test. Applying Fresnel's theory to the case of a shadow produced by a circular disk, Poisson deduced that the resulting diffraction pattern would have a bright spot at the center of the shadow—a result that was not predicted by any of the current particle theories, a result that no one involved had ever seen, and certainly a result that no one (least of all Poisson and his fellow committee members) expected. When the experiment was performed (by the chair of the evaluating committee, François Arago) and the bright spot actually appeared, resistance to Fresnel's theory collapsed, and he was awarded the Grand Prix. This was a major triumph for the wave theory of light. But notice that from the point of view of the received view of justification, the verified prediction of Poisson's bright spot should have provided no more justification to Fresnel's theory than did Fresnel's original deductions of known experimental results, and the behavior of the evaluation committee (which included, besides Poisson and Arago, other celebrated scientists of the time such as Pierre-Simon Laplace and Jean-Baptiste Biot) was quite unintelligible.

By the middle of the twentieth century, then, respected philosophers such as Popper and his followers complained that the received view of justification did not take into account the importance to scientific appraisal of novel predictions. But they also complained that the received view did not take into account other aspects of science relevant to scientific appraisal. These included, for example, the "fruitfulness" (Kuhn 1962, 1977) or "fertility" (McMullin 1968, 1976) or "progressiveness" (Lakatos 1970) of theories, that is, the inner resources theories exhibited over time for anticipating and dealing with the various empirical and conceptual problems that came their way. Imre Lakatos, for example, drew attention to the way Newtonian gravitational theory developed—how Newton first worked out his theory for a planetary system with a fixed, point-like sun and one single, point-like planet (from which he was able to derive his inverse square law for Kepler's ellipse), how he then replaced that model with one in which both sun and planet revolved around their common center of gravity, how he then worked out the model for more planets as if there were only heliocentric but no interplanetary forces, then worked out the case in which the sun and planets were not mass-points but mass-balls, then moved to spinning balls and their wobbles, then admitted interplanetary forces and started work on perturbations, then moved to bulging planets rather than round planets, and so on. These successive adjustments to Newton's theory were not random ad hoc changes forced on Newton by recalcitrant observational data but, rather, changes that were in some sense built into what Newton conceived as his theory right from the start, changes that were made independently of observational data. These changes, Lakatos argued, were part of the "positive heuristic" or original game plan of Newton's research program and, because they led to an ever more empirically accurate gravitational theory, they showed how very successful (fruitful, fertile, progressive) Newton's program was—"possibly the most successful research program ever" (Lakatos, 1970; and compare McMullin's treatment of the Bohr model of the hydrogen atom in McMullin 1968). That kind of success, Lakatos emphasized, cannot be appreciated by looking at only one version of a theory, as the received view was wont to do—even the most developed, most perfected, rationally reconstructed version of the theory—and comparing it with some particular array of observational data. That kind of success, urged Lakatos—and McMullin and Kuhn and others—can only be appreciated by looking at the theory over time, by looking at exactly how the theory develops and changes over time. In short, the unit of appraisal in science had to be not isolated theories but the temporally extended research programs that generated such theories.

There were, critics insisted, many other important aspects of scientific rationality left out of account by the views dominant in philosophy of science at mid-century. Stephen Toulmin (1953, 1961), Norwood Russell Hanson (1958), Dudley Shapere (1974), and Thomas Nickles (1978, 1980), for example, complained that the logical empiricist program in vogue at mid-century focused attention only on the results of scientific theorizing. Left out, as a consequence, were scientists' reasoning processes that had led to those results—for example, scientists' "abductive" or "retroductive" reasoning processes that led from their desire to explain puzzling data to the theories that seemed to offer the explanations, theories that thus merited further investigation (all of this, of course, had been eschewed by Reichenbach as part of what he deemed the philosophically irrelevant context of discovery rather than the philosophically important context of justification). Indeed, the logical empiricist picture focused only on results, never on the activities of scientists. It portrayed only the "logic of science": disembodied observations and observation statements; experiments detached from the individuals and groups who design them, fund them, and carry them out; scientific explanations detached from their proponents, their purposes, their audiences, their effects. Scientists themselves were nowhere to be seen. But only if we pay close attention to the activities of scientists, critics said—activities pertaining to discovery as well as justification—can we begin to learn about the scientific rationality logical empiricists were so keen to understand. So science's luminaries, such as Nicolaus Copernicus and Isaac Newton and Michael Faraday and James Clerk Maxwell and Antoine Lavoisier and Niels Bohr and, of course, the all-time favorite, Galileo Galilei, began to enjoy their fair share of philosophic attention, and Lakatos and his followers even set about to test theories of scientific rationality, such as his own methodology of scientific research programs, against the judgments of these greatest scientists (see, e.g., Howson 1976). At the same time, Kuhn and those he influenced focused attention on the dynamics of scientific communities, especially during periods of scientific change (such as the one described above involving Fresnel). And as time went on, the resources of cognitive science and social epistemology as well as the history and sociology of science were brought to bear on these projects.

It is worth noting in more detail the distinctive social framework that Kuhn provided for these studies of the activities of scientists. Whereas other philosophers started with individual (typically, highly successful) scientists, their methods and reasoning patterns and theoretical choices and the like, hoping to generalize to other scientists (to "scientists" in general), Kuhn's point of departure was scientific communities rather than individual scientists, and he explored the resources provided to these communities by the particular commonalities and differences he and others found among the individual scientists in them. Kuhn pointed out, for example, that agreement over fundamentals within a community (more particularly, agreement over a fundamental "paradigm theory" or set of paradigm theories) was a resource: it made possible the detailed, esoteric researches that characterized "mature" science, free of the endless clashes and challenges that stymied pre-paradigm science. Kuhn added, however, that diversity within a community could also be a resource. For example, although all scientists demand of the theories they accept that they satisfy certain basic criteria such as accuracy, simplicity, and fruitfulness, these criteria are individually imprecise and, when applied together, they repeatedly conflict (e.g., one theory might be simpler than another but also less accurate, or simpler in terms of the number or kinds of entities it postulates but more complex in terms of the mathematical operations it employs). In consequence, scientists fully committed to the same criteria for evaluating theories and making use of the same empirical data may nonetheless reach different conclusions when choosing between competing theories, especially at earlier stages of theory development, and this difference serves to minimize the risk of error for the community as a whole. The upshot was that philosophy of science's understanding of scientific rationality after Kuhn took account not only of individual scientists' activities (methods, reasoning patterns, theoretical choices, etc.) over time but also the social patterns to which these activities gave rise. Philosophy of science, in short, became socially informed on two levels of social analysis.

What, then, resulted from the mid-century critiques of philosophy of science? Certainly, many new philosophical/historical/psychological/ sociological insights regarding science resulted, as well as many new projects. But also, many new problems resulted, not the least of which was how to sort out the relations among the philosophy, history, and "sociology" (including psychology and anthropology) of science. (If one of the tasks of the philosophy of science, for example, was to articulate an acceptable empiricist methodology as part of scientific rationality, and one of the tasks of the *new* philosophy of science was to do this on the basis not of a priori rational reconstruction but of detailed research in the history and sociology of science, then was not an empiricist methodology already presupposed by the enterprise right from the start, and if so, what could be the basis of *that* methodology?) And finally, many new tools of philosophical analysis resulted from the mid-century critiques. Indeed, in the process of critique and response to critique, many of philosophy of science's most fundamental concepts were transformed. Basic dichotomies— between theory and observation, for example, or theory and practice—were dissolved: it became commonly acknowledged that observational claims were "theory-laden" and that theory both shaped and was shaped by observation and both shaped and was shaped by practice. What's more, basic categories of philosophical analysis changed their status: the heretofore near-algorithmic *criteria for the evaluation of theories*, for example, became the far more modest *epistemic* or *cognitive values*. Even the notion of scientific knowledge itself underwent fundamental change: from something purely propositional to something that could be learned "by finger exercises and by doing" but not be put into words, or not be put into words very easily (Kuhn 1970; see also Polanyi 1967); from something that could be expressed in language to something that could be embedded in language and, much later, embedded in other things as well, such as scientific instruments. And, of course, new historically and socially informed concepts such as *paradigm* and scientific *research program* came into use, and new historically and socially informed areas of investigation such as scientific experimentation came into vogue. (A paradigm theory, for example, was a concrete scientific achievement that was shared by a scientific community and was also what individuated one scientific community from another. Moreover, it directed scientific research in that community on many levels, not only by posing problems but also by providing standards for acceptable solutions to those problems.) Surely the success of philosophy of science's ambitious venture was finally assured.

A FURTHER OBSTACLE

There was one response—because there was one critique—that never appeared at mid-century, however. Through the efforts, particularly, of Kuhn, Hanson, Toulmin, Feyerabend, Lakatos, McMullin, and Shapere, together with all those they influenced, philosophy of science was "historicized" and "socialized" to make it more relevant to actual science; that is to say, philosophy of science was informed by analyses of the actual developmental processes of science and informed by analyses of the actual knowledge-productive social practices of science. But philosophy of science was not at the same time "contextualized"—that is, informed by analyses of the actual ways in which science interacts with the wider society in which it occurs, the ways in which science is shaped by and in turn shapes that society. The unit of analysis for philosophy of science remained (a historical, social) science in a vacuum.

True, there were a few scattered anticipations of a contextualized philosophy of science. Kuhn, for example, allowed that the wider social context of science could help to transform its anomalies into crisis-provoking problems and could even motivate the choice of a new theory, in just the way that the need for calendar reform in the sixteenth century made the factual difficulties confronting Ptolemaic astronomy more pressing and ultimately helped to bring about the transition to Copernican astronomy. After all, all theories, Kuhn explained, even the most empirically powerful theories, confront factual difficulties at all times. As a result, if theory change is to occur at all, then other factors than factual difficulties, such as the sheer length of time during which scientists have wrestled with a problem or the social importance of its solution, must precipitate that change. What's more, since the basic criteria of theory choice are individually imprecise and can jointly conflict, additional factors, including contextual factors, must intervene to help scientists make their choice. But once a theory has been chosen, the wider social context for Kuhn becomes quite irrelevant. The theory will then be able to direct future research single-handedly without the help of the social surround. Kuhn suggests, at any rate, that this kind of "paradigm-directed" science is the *normal* case in science, the *mature* case.[3] For others, however—for Lakatos (1970) and later for Larry Laudan (1977), for example[4]—the social shaping that precedes paradigm-directed science for Kuhn was "irrational," that is, contrary to what an acceptable theory of scientific rationality would sanction. Indeed, the test of a theory of scientific rationality for Lakatos was how much of actual science it "rationalized," that is, how little of actual science it suggested was socially influenced in this way (see Lakatos 1976). And

---

3. Ernan McMullin, too, would argue in the 1980s that social factors might play a role in the immature stages of a science but would be gradually sifted out with scientific advance. See McMullin 1983 and 1984; see also Hesse 1980.

4. And Newton-Smith 1981 and Shapere 1984.

these were the philosophers of science who actually considered the question of the wider society's shaping of science. For the rest, the question was never raised. And when it came to science's shaping of the wider society, the question was not even broached—by anyone.

It is strange that philosophy of science at mid-century conscientiously ignored the wider social context of science, since mid-century was a time when that context, at least in the United States, seemed to exert more than its usual share of influence on science (see, for what follows, Forman 1987; Kevles 1990; Leslie 1993; Geiger 1994; Hounshell 2001; and Solovey 2001). There was, to be sure, the massive military funding of science:

> In FY '38 the total U.S. budget for military research and development was $23 million and represented only 30% of all Federal R&D; in fiscal 1945 the OSRD [Office of Scientific Research and Development] alone spent more than $100 million, the Army and Navy together more than $700 million, and the Manhattan Project more than $800—an increase in current dollars over seven years by a factor of more than seventy, or more than fifty in constant dollars. In the immediate postwar years total military expenditure slumped to a mere seven times its prewar constant-dollar level, while constant-dollar military R&D expenditure held at a full 30 times its prewar level, and comprised about 90% of all Federal R&D. In the early 1950s total military expenditure soared again, reaching 20 times its prewar constant-dollar level, while military R&D reattained, and before the end of the decade much surpassed, its World War II high. (Forman 1987, 152)

And this massive military funding had profound effects on the science of the time and, in fact, on much of the science to come.

First, there were the more methodological and organizational effects, such as the shift from individual to group investigations and to investigations on a larger scale, utilizing more complex equipment and techniques, and the increased pressures for secrecy, classification, and restriction of access to research results, foreign travel, and professional association. In addition, there were the newly formed university-industry ties that enabled university laboratories to have greater access to defense contracts, more of which were going to the corporate sector.

Second, there were the more substantive effects. According to some (e.g., Forman 1987 and Leslie 1993), the massive military research funding diverted science away from basic research to military applications, deeply distorting scientific development in the process. According to others (e.g., Kevles 1990 and Geiger 1994), the massive military funding provided new opportunities for research and thereby enhanced scientific development in basic as well as applied research. For example, previously small subdisciplines of physics, such as electronics, aerospace engineering, nuclear physics, and materials science, grew into full-fledged, independent disciplines as they pursued defense-related research agendas. And according to still others (e.g., Solovey 2001 and Hounshell 2001), the massive military funding seriously compromised the objectivity of the science that resulted at least in the social sciences.

And third, there were the social effects. "The Pentagon virtually owned a number of fields that were critical to its missions"—electronics, aeronautical engineering, nuclear science, materials science, "and many others as well" (Geiger 1994, 630–631). As a result, some scientists in the early postwar years, and even into the early 1950s, deeply resented and actively condemned the enormously expanded military role science was then playing—"the degradation of the position of the scientist as an independent worker and thinker to that of a morally irresponsible stooge in a science-factory [of military weaponry]" (Norbert Wiener, quoted in Forman 1987, 185).

It is strange, then, that philosophy of science at mid-century conscientiously ignored the wider social context of science, since that context at just that time exerted especially strong effects on science and since the science that resulted exerted especially strong effects back—mostly via weapons-related products (missiles, atomic weapons) and weapons-related fears (air raid drills in schools, the construction of bomb shelters) but also via civilian goods such as televisions and computers. It is stranger still that philosophy of science did this after having done just the opposite earlier in the century. When we look back at the history of philosophy of science in the twentieth century, however, such a turnabout is exactly what recent historical scholarship suggests.

EARLY-TWENTIETH-CENTURY PHILOSOPHY OF SCIENCE: THE VIENNA CIRCLE

Most scholars of twentieth-century philosophy of science locate its roots in the Vienna Circle, that group of scientists, mathematicians, and scientists-turned-philosophers who regularly met in Vienna at the beginning of the twentieth century. The group counted among its members Moritz Schlick, Otto Neurath, Rudolf Carnap, Hans Hahn, Olga Hahn-Neurath, Philipp Frank, Friedrich Waismann, Kurt Gödel, and Herbert Feigl. And it counted as its task the construction of a "scientific conception of the world," a conception (in the words of the Vienna Circle's "manifesto")[5] "characterized not so much by theses of its own, but rather by its basic attitude, its points of view and direction of research." Its direction of research was clear: the overarching goal of the Vienna Circle was "unified science," "[a linking and harmonizing of] the achievements of individual investigators in their various fields of science." Hence the emphasis was on "collective efforts" and "what can be grasped intersubjectively," on the search for a "neutral system" of symbols and the clarity that can be gained through logical

5. The pamphlet "*Wissenschaftliche Weltauffassung: Der Wiener Kreis* [The Scientific Conception of the World: The Vienna Circle]," was popularly known as the Vienna Circle "manifesto." It was written by Neurath and edited by Carnap and Hahn. Others in the Vienna Circle were also asked for comments and contributions and gave them.

analysis (Carnap, Hahn, and Neurath [1929] 1973, 305–306). And what was eschewed was the disparate system building of traditional philosophers along with the "notion that *thinking* can . . . lead to knowledge out of its own resources without using any empirical material"—in short, "metaphysics" (308). In contrast with traditional philosophy, "the representatives of the scientific world-conception resolutely stand on the ground of simple human experience" because "there is no way to genuine knowledge other than the way of experience. . . . They confidently approach the task of removing the metaphysical and theological debris of millennia" and "returning . . . to a unified picture of this world." There is simply no other task for philosophy to do. This is the *"essence"* of the scientific conception of the world (316–317).

In pursuing this scientific conception of the world, however, the members of the Vienna Circle were motivated not only by abstract logical and epistemological concerns but by concrete social and political ones as well. "One cannot begin to give an account of the Vienna Circle without seeing it not only as a movement for a scientific world conception in terms of its logical, epistemological and methodological content, but also as a movement which conceived of its theoretical contributions as being in the service of social reform, and as, in significant measure, allied with the left social movements of its time" (Wartofsky 1996, 60).[6] Indeed, Philipp Frank, in his reminiscences of the Vienna Circle, noted that

> the whole original Viennese group was convinced that the elimination of metaphysics not only was a question of a better logic but was of great relevance for the social and cultural life. They were also convinced that the elimination of metaphysics would deprive the groups that we call today totalitarian of their scientific and philosophic basis and would lay bare the fact that these groups are actually fighting for special interests of some kind. (Frank 1949, 34)

Frank's own critique of the race theories of his day was a case in point. For example, he supplied numerous illustrations of the inconsistency with which the term *Aryan* was employed by the Nazis, concluding that the words *Aryan* and *non-Aryan* lacked "even any pretense of a relationship to a scientific race theory, and 'non-Aryan' simply meant anything that was antipathetic or dangerous to the ruling group" (Frank 1951, 105; Uebel 2003). At the same time, that "great task of anti-metaphysical empiricism" (Neurath [1935] 1983, 119), unity of science, was expected by the Vienna

6. Marx Wartofsky points out that many saw the Vienna Circle in this way, not only Neurath, Carnap, and Hahn but also, for example, Olga Hahn-Neurath and Philipp Frank; Bertrand Russell and Albert Einstein; critical philosophical colleagues such as Karl Popper; American students such as Ernest Nagel and Albert Blumberg; and even political enemies such as the right-wing Austro-German nationalists, the reactionary Catholic-clerical establishment in Vienna and in the university, and the proto-Nazis and anti-Semites, all of whom saw the Vienna Circle and its ideas as a social and political threat and not only as an intellectual one. Not everyone saw the Vienna Circle in this way, however. Schlick, for example, strongly disagreed with this characterization.

Circle not only to aid in the development of science but also to aid in the communication of its results to the public at large. It was expected, as well, to aid in the coordinated use of those results as tools for the deliberate shaping and planning of modern life. As Neurath proclaimed on the very first page of the first volume of the *International Encyclopedia of Unified Science*: "To further all kinds of scientific synthesis is one of the most important purposes of the unity of science movement, which is bringing together scientists in different fields and in different countries, as well as persons who have some interest in science or hope that science will help to ameliorate personal and social life" (Neurath 1938, 1). Planned "common action presses us toward a unified science" (Neurath [1931] 1973, 407).

For the Vienna Circle, then, philosophy of science was all about the construction of a scientific conception of the world, and that was all about the logical and epistemological analysis and synthesis of science in the service of progress, both scientific and social. "What characterises the modern scientific conception of the world is . . . the interconnection of empirical individual facts, with systematic testing by experiment, the joining of the individual into the texture of all sequences of events, and the uniform logical treatment of all trains of thought, in order to create a unified science that can successfully serve all transforming activity" (Neurath [1930] 1983, 42). Beyond this, however, the members of the Vienna Circle did not always see the role of philosophy of science in precisely the same way. For most of the Vienna Circle, what philosophy of science could or should contribute was purely theoretical, purely conceptual. In his "Intellectual Autobiography," Carnap put it this way: "Philosophy leads to an improvement in scientific ways of thinking and thereby to a better understanding of all that is going on in the world, both in nature and in society; this understanding in turn serves to improve human life" (Carnap 1963, 23–24). In particular, Carnap and the others "insisted that the intrusion of practical and especially of political points of view" was inappropriate and would, in fact, "violate the purity of philosophical methods":

> All of us in the Circle were strongly interested in social and political progress. Most of us, myself included, were socialists. But we liked to keep our philosophical work separated from our political aims. In our view, logic, including applied logic, and the theory of knowledge, the analysis of language, and the methodology of science, are, like science itself, neutral with respect to practical aims, whether they are moral aims for the individual, or political aims for a society. (Carnap 1963, 23)

How philosophy as well as science, understood in this purely neutral way, could be expected, nonetheless, to improve human life was never explained. After all, if philosophy and science were neutral with respect to practical aims, then, of course, pernicious practical aims could make use of these neutral resources to wreak havoc on human life just as easily as good practical aims could do just the opposite. Curiously, Carnap himself reported in the very same place: "We . . . defended the right to examine objectively and scientifically all processes or alleged processes without regard for the question of whether other people use or misuse the results" (Carnap 1963, 23).

Others in the Vienna Circle had a very different perspective. Neurath, in particular, Carnap tells us, criticized this neutralist stand as giving "aid and comfort to the enemies of social progress" (Carnap 1963, 23). The reasons are not far to seek. For Neurath, all knowledge of the world was, and always would be, full of uncertainty. To begin with, nothing in that knowledge could ever be foundational:

> Each attempt to create a world-picture by starting from a *tabula rasa* and making a series of statements which are recognized as definitively true, is necessarily full of trickeries. The phenomena that we encounter are so much interconnected that they cannot be described by a one-dimensional chain of statements. The correctness of each statement is related to that of all the others. It is absolutely impossible to formulate a single statement about the world without making tacit use at the same time of countless others. (Neurath 1913, 3)

As a result, "whoever wants to create a world-view or a scientific system must operate with doubtful premises" (Neurath 1913, 3), premises "alterable in principle" (Neurath 1934, 105).

But even if that were not the case—even if there *were* an independent and secure empirical foundation for science—the hypotheses constructed on that foundation, Neurath maintained, would still be doubtful. "Science is *ambiguous—and is so on each level.* . . . Poincare, Duhem and others have adequately shown that even if we have agreed on the protocol statements [the empirical foundation], there is an unlimited number of equally applicable, possible systems of hypotheses" (Neurath 1934, 105; translation amended). Moreover, there is an unlimited number of ways to unify whatever systems of hypotheses *are* accepted in the various sciences. In all these ways and others still,[7] Neurath insisted, scientists must cope with uncertainty, with questions and choices for which logic and empirical evidence are insufficient to provide answers. And hence, in all these ways, scientists may, and in fact *must*, bring to bear other kinds of considerations, including social and political considerations, to settle on answers in a fully objective science. While such external considerations are normally unconscious, the subject matter of historical, sociological, psychological, and even evolutionary biological investigations, there is no reason against their being fully conscious and deliberate. That is to say, there is no reason scientists should not consciously and deliberately direct their scientific choices, within the limits imposed by logic and empirical evidence, toward particular social and political ends and away from others. And Neurath argued that they should: "Successful collaboration is possible only when those who act fix on one possibility, whether by agreement or propaganda. This choice is itself a matter of action and resolution,

7. See Cartwright, Cat, Fleck, and Uebel 1996 for others.

but that does not mean that such action has no scientific basis" (Neurath [1928] 1973, 293).

As a result, Neurath advocated a more political role for philosophy of science and "often presented arguments of a more pragmatic-political rather than of a theoretical nature for the desirability or undesirability of certain logical or empirical investigations" (Carnap 1963, 23). In some ways this meant narrowing the array of questions and methods to be embraced by philosophy of science, but in other ways it meant broadening it to include socially and politically relevant topics such as the place of values in science, the sociology of science, and the logical and epistemological analysis of ideologies and ideological claims. And, of course, Neurath advocated (and did himself engage in) direct political action as well. "In the end Neurath outlined a theory of science that sought to provide the tools to empower its practitioners to intervene in, develop and newly create a social practice even under conditions 'not of their own choosing'"— "a tool for 'revolutionizing practice'" (Cartwright, Cat, Fleck, and Uebel 1996, 164–165; see also Reisch 2005 for more details).

Regardless of their different perceptions of the role of philosophy of science, however, the members of the Vienna Circle agreed about the significance of its results. Witness the concluding paragraph of the Vienna Circle manifesto:

> The scientific world-conception is close to the life of the present. Certainly it is threatened with hard struggles and hostility. Nevertheless there are many who do not despair but, in view of the present sociological situation, look forward with hope to the course of events to come. Of course not every single adherent of the scientific world-conception will be a fighter. Some, glad of solitude, will lead a withdrawn existence on the icy slopes of logic: some may even disdain mingling with the masses and regret the "trivialized" form that these matters take on spreading. However, their achievements too will take a place among the historic developments. We witness the spirit of the scientific world-conception penetrating in growing measure the forms of personal and public life, in education, upbringing, architecture and the shaping of economic and social life according to rational principles. *The scientific world-conception serves life, and life receives it.* (Carnap, Hahn, and Neurath [1929] 1973, 317–318)

And life did receive it. The Vienna Circle played a valuable role in the *Volksbildung* (adult education) movement and in the general cultural life of Vienna, and although its voice remained a minority one in official academia, it commanded a serious following among "a relatively large part of the Vienna intelligentsia," by one report (Uebel 1998, 422; Bergmann [1938] 1993). The Vienna Circle had serious followings, as well, in Prague, Berlin, Lwow, Warsaw, and New York. Regarding the last, the Vienna Circle (especially Neurath and Carnap) and New York left-leaning intellectuals (such as John Dewey, Ernest Nagel, and Sidney Hook)

> stimulated and nourished each other, providing resources, credibility, and epistemological muscle to fight their battles. For example, Dewey's sleepy

and relentlessly general discussions promoting science as social, organized intelligence in the service of social and cultural progress were empowered by Hook's and Nagel's polemics that drew on [the Vienna Circle's] bold dichotomies between metaphysics and science, antiquated rationalism and modern empiricism, and its main conception of science as a unified whole. (Reisch 2005, 82)

"Until Austro-Fascism and Nazism put an end to the experiment in democracy, 'life' did receive, to some degree at least, the scientific world-conception" (Uebel 1998, 422).

By the middle of the twentieth century, however, neither the Vienna Circle nor its scientific world conception was able to play any significant role at all, either in science or in social life. The concern with unified science had degenerated from an active movement—seeking to regularize collaboration among scientists from different countries and different academic fields for the improvement of both science and human life—to an academic thesis—a hypothesis concerning the future internal development of science "viewed, so to speak, from across the quadrangle as an independent intellectual project neither requiring nor requesting input from philosophy" (Reisch 2005, 375). And that which had been categorically eschewed by the Vienna Circle—the "notion that *thinking* can . . . lead to knowledge out of its own resources without using any empirical material"—now seemed embraced in the expectation that the conceptual analysis of such ideas as *scientific law*, *scientific explanation*, and *scientific justification* would provide insight into the actual workings of science. By the time it had become institutionalized as the mainstream in philosophy of science in the United States and elsewhere, as the "standard view" or "received view," the contextualized philosophy of the Vienna Circle had been transformed into the uncontextualized philosophy of science already described. What had happened?

A variety of explanations have been offered (see, for various accounts, Giere 1999; McCumber 2001; Howard 2003; and Reisch 2005). For one thing, the primary shapers and spokespersons of the Vienna Circle's philosophy of science after the war—most prominently, Carnap, Reichenbach, and Hempel—tended to be just those members or followers of the Vienna Circle who "liked to keep [their] philosophical work separated from [their] political aims"—"on the icy slopes of logic." Neurath, the "locomotive" of the Vienna Circle, did not survive the war; nor could his writings speak for him, since they were not available in English translation until many years later (*Empiricism and Sociology* in 1973 and *Philosophical Papers 1913–1946* in 1983). Indeed, "the development of Logical Empiricism in North America proceeded in virtual ignorance of the major early writings that defined the European movement" (Giere 1999, 220). What's more, the North American social/political context in which Carnap, Reichenbach, and other philosophers of science found themselves after the war[8] was much more stable, democratic, and liberal than that of prewar German-speaking Europe, much less evocative of the reformist zeal of the Vienna Circle. Conceptualizing science and the philosophy of science within this new context as sources of social transformation must have seemed increasingly out of place, especially within a growing ideological climate that extolled "pure science" as a source of "knowledge for its own sake" (see, e.g., Bush 1945 and Schweber 2000). And the addition of McCarthyism to that context in the 1950s must have magnified the dis-ease: the public record "clearly indicates that philosophy was the most heavily attacked of all the academic disciplines" (McCumber 2001, 37), a situation that a decontextualization and depoliticization of philosophy might well have ameliorated. Finally, the developments in the field of philosophy of science in the 1950s alluded to earlier—new departments, centers, and programs for the philosophy of science; new journals and book and conference series; expanded governmental and private foundation funding for research; and growing prominence of philosophy of science within philosophy proper—must have further encouraged the movement away from social engagement:

> A more avowedly political posture is to be expected from a discipline that stands on the margins of the academy and the cultural establishment, as did logical empiricism and scientific philosophy in Europe in the 1920s and 1930s. . . . A drift to the political center and toward political neutrality often accompanies a discipline's establishing itself among the cultural institutions of the day, not so much because the members of the discipline change their views as because a discipline at the cultural center attracts relatively more of its new members from the politically and culturally less alienated segments of the population. (Howard 2003, 72)

Doubtless there were other factors at play as well. What these various accounts do not explain, however, is why philosophy of science continued to ignore the wider social context of science right through to the end of the century. By the end of the twentieth century, after all, even the mass media was rife with evidence of the influence of society on science and science on society: the suppression of scientific studies and scientific findings by industry and government alike and the turning of research results into "intellectual property" to be kept secret for commercial purposes; the initiation of agricultural or medical or economic or military policies worldwide as a result of particular scientific projects and the initiation of particular scientific projects in response to commercial or political objectives;

8. Or, at least in the case of Reichenbach, anticipated. Giere points out (1999, 206) that Reichenbach began exploring the possibility of emigrating to the United States even before he began teaching at the University of Berlin in 1927, and that in 1933, when Reichenbach was dismissed with the imposition of the Nazi racial laws, he shifted his research focus and even the language of his writing accordingly.

self-promoting scientific press releases that bypass the usual scientific literatures in order to have a quicker, more dramatic effect as well as other kinds of popularizations of scientific findings that shape public opinion; the financial interests scientists have in specific kinds of scientific projects and scientific results; and so on. And the other areas of science studies had already generated a sizable literature on this mutual shaping of science and society under such headings as the "commercialization of science," the "politicization of science," "post-academic science," and "Mode 2" (see, e.g., Gibbons et al. 1994; Ziman 2000a and 2000b; Nowotny, Scott, and Gibbons 2001). Why were philosophers of science lagging so far behind? Indeed, why are *we* philosophers of science now in the twenty-first century *still* lagging so far behind? Do we have any good reasons to do so?

DIAGNOSTIC REFLECTIONS

One reason we give for our persistent failure to situate science within its wider social context when philosophizing about science is that our concerns lie—have always lain—with the context of scientific justification, not with the context of discovery or the context of application. So we can safely ignore the wider society in which science occurs, we claim, because that society relates only to the context of discovery and the context of application, not to the context of justification. But just what do we mean by *justification* here? When Hans Reichenbach proclaimed his famous context of discovery/context of justification distinction and urged philosophers of science to follow him in concerning themselves only with the latter, he did not mean by justification, as we have seen, the actual deliberative practices in which scientists engage. Those actual practices were, for Reichenbach, the province of the psychology and sociology of science, not the philosophy of science; they belonged to the context of discovery, not the context of justification. What Reichenbach meant by justification, remember, was a "logical substitute" for what actually happens, "a better way of thinking than actual thinking," a "rational reconstruction" (Reichenbach 1938, 3–8). But nowadays—now that our efforts to historicize and socialize philosophy of science have borne fruit—nowadays when we philosophers of science say that our concerns lie with the context of justification, what most of us mean by justification is much closer to the actual deliberative practices of Reichenbach's context of discovery than to his context of justification. And when we study those actual deliberative practices, we at least sometimes find that they are sensitive to the wider social context of the science in question. We sometimes find, for example, that scientists count as a factor in favor of a theory, or even as a constraint on their theorizing, that their theory helps to promote a more egalitarian society or at least that their theory does not help to promote a less egalitarian society. We sometimes find, for example, that scientists studying the development of sexual orientation adopt as a constraint on their theorizing that

nonheterosexual orientations not be pathologized or that scientists studying domestic violence adopt as a constraint on their theorizing that racial
stereotypes not be perpetuated (see, e.g., West 2002 and Horvath 2004).
Why, then, are our philosophical understanding of scientific justification
and our philosophical picture of science in general not similarly sensitive
to the wider social context of science?

Another reason we give for not philosophizing about the unit science-
in-society is closely connected to this first one. It relates to science's aim.
The aim of science, we philosophers say, is truth—or empirical adequacy,
or empirical success, or explanatory success, or something of the sort—
and science progresses by accumulating such truths or successes. Being
sensitive to the wider social context of science does not, or at least need
not, advance this aim or contribute to this progress. That a theory helps to
promote a more egalitarian society, for example, is not relevant to the
theory's truth or empirical success. So it should not be a factor in what we
philosophers take to be the scientific justification of the theory, even if
scientists sometimes count it as such. And more generally, sensitivity to
the wider social context of science, to its funding as well as its social
effects, for example, should not be part of our philosophical concerns
about science.

The problem with this second reason for ignoring the wider social context of science lies with its conception of the aim of science. Determining
what the aim of science is requires a great deal of information, information that tends to be absent from philosophical discussions (see Kourany
2000 for a fuller treatment). Indeed, determining what the aim of science
is requires *empirical* information, because the task it sets is to best interpret *science*, an actually existing activity, not an activity whose nature it is
up to us to dream up. And determining what the aim of science is requires
normative information, because the task it sets is to *best interpret* science,
to interpret it so that it makes the most sense, is the most reasonable or
rational—what science (in this case, the aim of science) *ought* to be.

Start with the empirical. In order to determine how best to interpret
the aim of science, we need empirical data regarding what *scientists* (as
against philosophers) say the aim of science is, or at least what scientists
say the aim of their science is—scientists past and present—or, better still,
what scientists say *their aim* as scientists is. (Many researchers within the
health sciences, for example, say that the aim of these sciences is the oblit-
eration of disease and infirmity, while many others say that it is the production of "complete physical, mental, and social well-being," to use the
World Health Organization's characterization, which might differ for
people of different race, class, gender, and other characteristics. Many
political scientists, by contrast, say that the aim of political science, or at
least their aim as political scientists, is to obtain policy-relevant information for heads of state and such organizations as Greenpeace and Amnesty
International and the CIO.) More important for our purposes, however, is
what scientists have actually aimed at in their research. Relevant here is

what scientists have said they were aiming at, but also who was funding their research and why they were funding it, who was evaluating that research (e.g., the way it uses animals) and why they were evaluating it, where that research would be published, and who would stand to profit from it and how. (What was being aimed at in the famous cloning experiments on Dolly the sheep, for example, can be variously interpreted as "basic understanding," or greater agricultural or biotechnological or medical efficiency, or money.)

In order to determine how best to interpret the aim of science, then, we need to take into account empirical data such as these. But we also need to take into account normative considerations. These include the empirical underdetermination of theories, the nature of the observational-theoretical distinction, and the other issues habitually brought up in the realism/antirealism controversy that help to determine what the aim of science *ought* to be (see, e.g., van Fraassen 1980). But they also include other kinds of normative considerations. After all, society ultimately pays for science, and society is deeply affected by science. Hence the needs of society, including the justice-related needs of society, and the ways science might satisfy those needs are also relevant when determining what the aim of science ought to be. Relevant here, for example, are the political aims of sociologists who research environmental racism, or the commercial and political aims behind the absence of research on the effects of pesticides and fertilizers on migrant farm workers, or the moral aims of the animal-rights activists who have obstructed the use of long-accepted biological research methods, or the moral and religious aims of the antiabortionists who have blocked fetal and embryo research.

Only if we philosophers of science take into account both kinds of considerations, both empirical and normative considerations, can we hope to gain an adequate understanding of the aim or aims of science and, thereby, the methods and modes of assessment that are appropriate to science, the genuine progress it has achieved and has hope of achieving, and other central issues in the philosophy of science. But, of course, taking into account those empirical and normative considerations—regarding the funding of science and the social needs science should serve and the rest—*is* to situate science within its wider social context when philosophizing about science.

This inspires a third reason we give for not situating science within its wider social context. This third reason reflects on *our* aims rather than the aims we impute to scientists. Our aim as philosophers of science, we say, is to understand science as a knowledge-producing activity, even if science is other things as well. Our interests, after all, are epistemological, not social or political. We are *epistemologists* of science, nothing else. So what is important to us in our various inquiries about science is whether scientists' methods are epistemically appropriate, whether their claims are epistemically justified, whether their research results make epistemic progress, not whether and in what ways these are socially motivated or socially worthwhile. In short, we philosophers of science simply do not need to be sensitive to the wider social context of science when philosophizing about science, since that wider social context is irrelevant to our concerns.

The problem with this third reason for ignoring the social context of science is that it is self-defeating. Assume for the moment that our aims regarding science are solely epistemological.[9] Even then, the wider social context of science—the funding sources of scientists, the secrecy requirements surrounding selected scientific results, the pressures exerted on scientists by various interest groups (feminists, gay-rights activists, animal-rights activists), and so forth—poses epistemological questions we cannot afford to ignore. Take the effects that activists representing AIDS patients have had on biomedical research related to AIDS—for example, activists' effects on the design and interpretation of randomized clinical trials (see, for this example, Epstein 1996). Critiquing what they called "pure" or "clean" or "elegant" science pursuing its leisurely course in the midst of an AIDS epidemic, AIDS activists pushed for and achieved such changes as expanded access to clinical trials so that AIDS patients could be enrolled in more than one trial at a time or could be taking concomitant medications while enrolled in a single trial, more rapid movement of compounds into clinical trials, and acceleration of the drug-approval process. Were these changes epistemically progressive, yielding better knowledge because they effectively responded to the needs and desires of AIDS patients, or were they epistemically regressive, yielding worse knowledge because they gave up on claims to universal validity in favor of a validity that was more local and circumscribed? This is a "real world" epistemological question that has divided the AIDS activist community. It is, moreover, an urgent epistemological question because now other groups—Alzheimer's patients, multiple-sclerosis patients, breast-cancer patients, and a host of others—have been pressing for or achieving some of the same kinds of changes as the AIDS activists (in former NIH director Bernadine Healy's words, "The AIDS activists have led the way. . . . [They] have created a template for all activist groups looking for a cure" [quoted in Epstein 1996, 348]). This question about the epistemic effects of the changes wrought by AIDS activists is, however, not only an urgent practical question; it is also an important theoretical question, because the mode of experimentation that is being transformed by the changes— randomized clinical trials—has been for quite some time now the "gold standard" in medicine, central to medicine's legitimation as a fully scientific discipline. This urgent, theoretically important, real-world epistemological question is the kind of question to which we philosophers of science are equipped to provide answers, but it is also the kind of question

---

9. This assumption will be challenged in the chapters to follow.

to which we philosophers of science will not be able to provide answers unless we take into account the wider social context of science.

PROGNOSTIC REFLECTIONS

But what is in the offing if we do make efforts to contextualize philosophy of science? First note what is *not* in the offing. Abstract logico-mathematical analysis in such areas as philosophy of physics, philosophy of mathematics, and philosophy of biology will *not* disappear from philosophy of science, nor will it be discounted or downgraded in importance. Why should it? Such work can and often does fulfill important roles in both philosophy of science and the sciences—can and often does fulfill these roles even in the midst of the efforts that have been made to historicize and socialize philosophy of science. Indeed, abstract logico-mathematical analysis often enriches and is enriched by historical and/or social analysis, and there is no reason to suppose that abstract logico-mathematical analysis will not similarly enrich and be enriched by contextual analysis. At the same time, a philosophy of science that takes into account the wider social context of science, including the needs and resources of that wider social context, will have to reflect that context not only in its substantive work but also in its priorities. Such a philosophy of science will strive to cover the issues of greatest social concern. So while abstract work in such areas as philosophy of physics, philosophy of mathematics, and philosophy of biology will not disappear from a contextualized philosophy of science or be discounted or downgraded in importance, work in such areas as philosophy of the social and behavioral sciences and philosophy of medicine will need to become much more prominent in the field—more encouraged in philosophy of science curricula and conferences and publications, and more rewarded.

So much for what is not in the offing. Turn now to what is. Locating science within its wider social context reveals how scientific rationality is shaped or constrained by that wider context—by the pressures exerted by AIDS activists or other interest groups, for example, or industry or government. Since the goal of philosophy of science is to articulate scientific rationality, then philosophers of science will need to pay close attention to that wider social context and the effects it has on science. But since the goal of philosophy of science is also to aid in the development of scientific rationality, then philosophers of science will need to assess the legitimacy of those societal effects on science. To get some sense of the possibilities here, consider the controversy regarding the "politicization of science" that has been very much in the news. Some years back (in July 2003), two conservative U.S. think tanks, the Hoover Institution at Stanford University and the George C. Marshall Institute in Washington, D.C., published a collection of essays entitled *Politicizing Science: The Alchemy of Policymaking* (Gough 2003). The authors of the essays—scientists who had participated in or witnessed firsthand the interactions of politics and science—provided a series of examples suggesting that the science that informs U.S. policy making has been manipulated, distorted, or suppressed to advance liberal causes, to the detriment of society. "The more that political considerations dominate scientific considerations," warned the editor, biologist Michael Gough, "the greater the potential for policy driven by ideology and less based on strong scientific underpinnings" (Gough 2003, 3). The next month (in August 2003), U.S. Congressman Henry Waxman, a liberal Democrat, released a report detailing another series of examples of political manipulation, distortion, or suppression of science. This time, however, the report, entitled *Politics and Science in the Bush Administration* (U.S. House of Representatives 2003), suggested that the science that informs U.S. policy making has been manipulated to advance conservative causes. The Waxman report was followed six months later (in February 2004, updated in March 2004) by *Scientific Integrity in Policymaking: An Investigation into the Bush Administration's Misuse of Science*, issued by the Union of Concerned Scientists (2004b), and by *Restoring Scientific Integrity in Policy Making*, a condemnation of the Bush administration's political interference with science signed by 62 eminent scientists, including 20 Nobel laureates (Union of Concerned Scientists 2004a). And these were followed two months later (in April 2004) by presidential science advisor John Marburger's denial of the charges (Marburger 2004). What all these publications had in common was a view of science as a disinterested force that can guide policy making by providing appropriate facts, but only so long as science is kept separate from politics. As the Union of Concerned Scientists put it: "Science and scientific knowledge have played a large part in the policies that have made the United States the world's most powerful nation and its citizens increasingly prosperous and healthy. For science to play this positive and rational role in governance, the processes through which science influences government must be free of distortion and misrepresentation" (Union of Concerned Scientists 2004b, 29).

Not everyone in the controversy shared this view, however. Consider one kind of politicization that was at issue, that of screening scientific experts regarding their political views before they are invited to serve on scientific advisory committees and replacing such scientific experts when their political views come into conflict with the preferred political views. Representative Waxman, the Union of Concerned Scientists, and the scientists who signed *Restoring Scientific Integrity in Policy Making* all accused the Bush administration of politicizing science in this way—for example, by asking candidates for advisory committee vacancies whether they voted for President Bush or whether they agreed with the Bush administration's policies—and until April 2005, Science Advisor Marburger consistently denied these charges.[10] But

10. Marburger finally admitted that the Bush administration had politicized science in this way in the session on "Scientific Integrity in Government" at the April 2005 meeting of the American Physical Society. He also promised that the Bush administration would discontinue the practice.

some administration sympathizers claimed that such politicization was understandable and appropriate. Thus, one of the participants in a March 2004 Marshall Institute Roundtable on politicizing science, political scientist Steven Hayward, said: "When you win elections, you get to hire the people you want to work for you"; "the suggestion that the Administration shouldn't be able to hire the people they want to hire and [shouldn't be able to] not hire the people that [a left-leaning organization like] the Union of Concerned Scientists wants them to hire smacks of . . . political naiveté" (Kieper et al. 2004).

At the same time, another observer, geologist and director of Arizona State University's Consortium for Science, Policy, and Outcomes Daniel Sarewitz, pointed out that representatives of different scientific specialties bring to an advisory committee different disciplinary orientations, including different methods, standards of proof, interests, and values, as well as different bodies of knowledge, and thus far in the development of science such differences among specialties have become increasingly marked. This increasing disunity within science "translates into a multitude of different yet equally legitimate scientific lenses for understanding and interpreting nature," some more congenial to one political perspective, some more congenial to another (Sarewitz 2004, 390). The ongoing debate over genetically modified organisms in agriculture is an obvious case in point, with, on the one side, plant geneticists and molecular biologists at once concerned with understanding and controlling the attributes of specific organisms and allied with the politics of the agricultural biotechnology industry and, on the other side, ecologists and population biologists concerned with the complexity, interconnectedness, and lack of predictability of nature and allied with the politics of environmentalists. The upshot is that even without asking candidates for scientific advisory committee vacancies whom they voted for or whose policies they support, decisions on their candidacy can still be political.

Still another observer, political scientist David Guston, said that *no* way of choosing scientific advisory committee members is politically neutral—not only because different disciplinary orientations tend to be aligned with different political perspectives but also because scientists' credentials tend to be tied to the politics of government or industry funding as well as the politics of journal publishing, among other things (see, for an interesting case regarding the last, McCook 2005). As a result, the whole question regarding the politicization of science was unproductive. "Asking whether science is politicized distracts us from asking, 'Who benefits and loses from which forms of politicization?'" (Guston 2004, 25). We thereby neglect the more critical question of how science *should* be politicized. To this revised question, however, many had already provided answers. Some had suggested that science should be politicized in a bipartisan way rather than in the partisan way in which the Bush administration was proceeding, or at least in a way that was more balanced between Congress and the Executive Branch (by reestablishing the Congressional Office of Technology Assessment, for example). But others envisioned a more directly democratic form of politicization. Guston himself, for example, suggested that current rules guiding the formation and functioning of science advisory committees—current rules for deciding who the experts are (including conflict-of-interest provisions), what kinds of evidence and other considerations they may bring to their deliberations, and how they may settle their disagreements—should be opened to public scrutiny and evaluation and further articulation. And the application of these rules should be a matter of public accountability as well. More than that, he suggested that the public's advice should be integrated with scientific experts' advice. "One could imagine building the capacity to foster exchanges among experts, citizens, and civic organizations at all major research universities—not to replace more technocratic methods, but as a necessary complement for a system of democratic science advice, analysis and assessment" (Guston 2004, 28). Such participatory mechanisms, he added, are already in place in Europe.

For Sarewitz (2004), however, the critical question we needed to deal with was not how should science be politicized but, rather, how should politics be descientized. The reason was that nature is so complex that a variety of different disciplines is needed to investigate most aspects of it. Think of global climate change, for example—which can be variously understood as a problem of climate impacts, weather impacts, biodiversity, land use, energy production and consumption, agricultural productivity, public health, economic development patterns, material wealth, demographic patterns, and so forth. The rub is that, as pointed out previously, the different disciplines bring with them different, even incompatible, methods, standards of proof, interests, and values, as well as different, even incompatible, bodies of knowledge. Conversely, different value perspectives may find in such diverse bodies of scientific information different supporting facts and theories. The upshot, said Sarewitz, was that progress in addressing the environmental issues such as global climate change—and doubtless the health issues as well—that were the main focus of the politicization controversy "will need to come primarily from advances in political process, rather than scientific research" (Sarewitz 2004, 399), since scientific research can be used "to support entirely different interpretations of what is going on, and entirely different courses of action for how to address what is going on" (389). This did not mean that science should disappear from the scene. But it did mean that science should take "its rightful place as one among a plurality of cultural factors that help determine how people frame a particular problem or position—it is a part of the cognitive ether, and the claim to special authority vanishes" (400).

Meanwhile, the controversy continued. In July 2004, the Union of Concerned Scientists published yet another investigation of the Bush administration's interference with science (2004c), and since then it has published a variety of additional reports. What's more, by 2008 more than 15,000 scientists had signed *Restoring Scientific Integrity in Policy Making*, including 52 Nobel laureates, 63 National Medal of Science recipients, and 195 members of the National Academy of Sciences. In addition, books and articles and news stories and conference sessions continued to focus on the politicization of science, and many said that the future of U.S. public policy, and even, in significant ways, U.S. science, hung in the balance. But U.S. philosophers of science remained silent—despite the fact that philosophers of science and their colleagues in related areas of philosophy were far from silent through much of the twentieth century about such topics as the relations between facts and values, the underdetermination of theory by fact, the epistemic requirements for belief versus the practical requirements for action, and the relations among the contexts of discovery, justification, and application. This silence would have been understandable if the controversy had been merely political, merely a partisan battle between the liberal Union of Concerned Scientists and the conservative Bush administration and its supporters, for example, or between the conservative scientist-authors of *Politicizing Science: The Alchemy of Policymaking* and the liberal Clinton administration. And, of course, there is some reason to think that the controversy *was* merely political. After all, if the issue at stake were really the politicization of science, then why did the Union of Concerned Scientists not critique the Clinton administration's politicization of science, and why did the authors of *Politicizing Science* not similarly critique the Bush administration's far more blatant politicization of science?

But was the politicization controversy merely political? To think that it was is to think that the distinguished scientists who wrote *Politicizing Science* and the distinguished Nobel laureates, National Academy of Sciences members, and the like who signed *Restoring Scientific Integrity in Policy Making* (and who included Republicans as well as Democrats, and advisors in previous Republican as well as Democratic administrations) were either utterly confused or were lying. Surely there are more plausible— and more charitable—ways to think about the controversy. One such way is to think of the politicization controversy as simply another skirmish in the larger Science Wars. After all, the politicization of science controversy, as even the above quick glimpse suggests, covers a spectrum of positions—from politics should be kept out of the science that informs public policy, to politics can properly shape such science, to politics inevitably shapes such science, to such science should be kept out of the politics that informs public policy, at least until that politics can be worked out. And this spectrum maps onto the scientific-realist value-free science/ scientific-relativist social-constructivist spectrum of the Science Wars debates. Still another, even more plausible approach to the politicization controversy is to think of it as just what it seemed: a reflection of serious attempts all around to ensure that U.S. public policy has the best kind of basis it can have. If either of these alternative understandings of the politicization controversy is acceptable, however, then philosophers' silence on the controversy was an embarrassment. For then the issues that lie at the heart of the controversy were epistemological ones—just the kind we philosophers of science take to define our field. A contextualized philosophy of science would have enabled us to do our fair share toward resolving this controversy, and surely we should have done no less. This suggests just one of the good things in store if we do make efforts to contextualize philosophy of science.

THERAPEUTIC REFLECTIONS

But how do we contextualize philosophy of science—how do we take into account the wider social context of science when philosophizing about science? Fortunately, we do not have to start from scratch. Feminist philosophers of science, in collaboration with feminist historians and sociologists of science and feminist scientists themselves, have been pursuing a comprehensive analysis of science in society for years. They have thus given us a model for how to do it—a model that now awaits our attention. . . .

3

What Feminist Science Studies
Can Offer

If philosophers of science could ignore the wider social context of science for much of the twentieth century, *feminist* philosophers of science could not. That wider social context, after all, was the site of inequality for women—inequality in jobs, inequality in wages, inequality in expectations and treatment both in the home and outside it—and science, feminists were discovering, was helping to perpetuate that inequality. Never mind the history of misogyny in the research output of such fields as psychology and biology. Never mind the history of women's neglect in the research output of other fields such as economics and medical research. Never mind the appalling lack of opportunities for women or downright exclusion of women as practitioners in the histories of all the sciences. The jarring fact was that it was all continuing even at the end of the twentieth century. Rather than helping the cause of equality—by replacing prevailing ignorance and prejudice and misinformation about women with more adequate perspectives—science was doing just the opposite. If combating androcentrism and sexism in society was the first order of business for feminists, combating androcentrism and sexism in science was surely the first order of business for those feminists who were philosophers of science. But how?

The task demanded interdisciplinary collaboration and received it. Feminist scientists and historians of science exposed sexism and androcentrism in such fields as anthropology, sociology, political science, medical research, psychology, biology, and archaeology, and they exposed, as well, the obstacles female scientists faced in those and other fields. And feminist philosophers of science, along with feminist scientists and historians, investigated the actions that needed to be taken in response. What resulted was not only a rich array of resources for dealing with sexism and androcentrism in science—and, by extension, racism and heterosexism and classism and the like—but also an important set of beginnings for generating a contextualized (and even, as we shall see, a politicized) philosophy of science.

THE METHODOLOGICAL APPROACH TO
SEXISM IN SCIENCE

Doubtless the earliest mode of response to androcentrism and sexism in science came from feminist scientists. Many of these scientists pointed out that a great deal of androcentric and sexist science was, by the lights of traditional scientific methodology, simply bad science—science that failed to satisfy accepted standards of concept formation or experimental design or data analysis or the like (see, e.g., Hubbard 1979; Bleier 1984; Fausto-Sterling 1985). If only such standards were rigorously followed, it was suggested, the problems of sexism and androcentrism in science would be, at the very least, much reduced.

The whole issue of premenstrual syndrome (PMS) was a case in point. By the 1980s, PMS had become a biomedical problem of significant proportions. Estimated by some to affect as many as 80, 90, or even 100 percent of all women, it had by then been linked to impaired concentration, impaired physical coordination, impaired judgment, decreased efficiency, and lower performance in school and at work. PMS had even been linked to deviant behavior and diminished moral and legal responsibility. In two sensational murder trials in the United Kingdom, for example, the courts found PMS to justify reduced sentences on the grounds of the defendants' impaired capacity to control their behavior. The conclusion drawn from all this, of course, was that women, due to their reproductive biology, were less capable than men of holding positions of power and responsibility in society (Rittenhouse 1991; Easteal 1991; Chrisler and Caplan 2002).

Yet the science that supported this conclusion was deeply flawed. To begin with, there was no agreed-upon definition of PMS. Instead, PMS was variously linked to a very large number of "symptoms"—headaches, epilepsy, depression, dizziness, hoarseness, asthma, nausea, constipation, bloating, increased or decreased appetite, low blood sugar, joint and muscle pains, heart palpitations, glaucoma, skin disorders, breast tenderness, and a host of others (100 to 150 in all)—and none of these nor any combination of them was taken to be a necessary or definitive diagnostic sign of PMS. Moreover, most of these conditions were ones that everyone experienced from time to time, conditions that did not necessarily indicate any disease state at all, much less the specific disease state that PMS was supposed to be. Nor was there agreement regarding how severe these symptoms had to be in order to count as PMS. As a result, a woman suffering from a few low days and a woman suffering from suicidal depression might both be diagnosed as having PMS. And there was no agreement, as well, regarding the necessary timing of the symptoms. Thus, some studies of PMS looked only at the day or two preceding menstruation, while others looked at the week preceding, and still others looked at the two weeks preceding (i.e., the entire luteal phase, from ovulation until the start of menstruation). Some studies included some or all of the menstrual phase as well. And there were other problems. For example, most researchers were unable to ascertain which phase of the menstrual cycle their subjects were actually in at the time when symptoms were being monitored, since, among other reasons, menstrual cycles are not all of the same length.[1] And when researchers eliminated as subjects women with infrequent or variable cycles, choosing instead to focus only on those women with ideal, regular, 28-day menstrual cycles, they ended up gathering data on a very skewed segment of the overall population. The frequent absence of (male or anovulatory, amenorrheic, premenarcheal, or postmenopausal female) control groups was also a problem, since without such controls, it was impossible to determine if reported symptoms were a function of the menstrual cycle rather than other factors. The result of all of these problems and others besides was that no conclusion regarding women's lesser capabilities could be validly drawn from this research. Not only were the individual studies flawed, but there was also little comparability among them to help compensate for those flaws (Parlee 1973; Abplanalp 1983; Fausto-Sterling 1985; Chrisler and Caplan 2002).

Equally serious methodological problems beset the sexist and androcentric research described in chapter 1. It was there pointed out, for example, that until the 1990s, diseases such as heart disease that affect both sexes were defined as male diseases, studied primarily in white, middle-aged, middle-class males, and clinically handled accordingly. As a result, heart disease in women (who, as it turns out, differ from men in symptoms, patterns of disease development, and reactions to treatment) was often not detected and not properly managed when it was detected. Such problems could be—and ultimately were—handled simply by following accepted methodological procedures, such as designing clinical studies with groups of subjects that were more nearly representative of the patient population at large (see, e.g., Rosser 1994 and "Women's Health Research" 1995). Similarly, at least many of the problems relating to PMS could have been handled simply by following such accepted methodological procedures as designing appropriate controls and measurement procedures (e.g., screening subjects for other medical or psychiatric disorders that may influence their PMS symptom profile). One survey (Chrisler and Caplan 2002) suggests that this is still not being done.

For many feminist scientists of the past, then, rigorously applying accepted standards of good science was the way to eliminate at least much

---

1. The most commonly used method to determine cycle phase—the calendar method—was also the least reliable. Researchers would count ahead from the date of a subject's last menstrual period to the date that they would estimate would mark the subject's next premenstrual phase. This method assumed not only that a subject's menstrual cycles would all be of the same length (despite fluctuations in life stresses etc.) but also that a subject would have a reliable memory of the date of her last period. The most precise method, on the other hand—hormonal assay—was also the least commonly used due to its expense (because behavioral-science researchers lack training in biochemistry, they have to hire others to do the assays) (Chrisler and Caplan 2002).

of the sexism and androcentrism in science. For some of the feminist scientists, however, those accepted standards needed quite a bit of refurbishing in order to meet the goal. Feminist sociologist Margrit Eichler (1988), for example, proposed a set of "guidelines for nonsexist research" to supplement what science students and researchers were already expected to live up to. Her guidelines covered all aspects of the research process, from the title right down to the policy recommendations that might follow from the research results, and they included such items as the following regarding research concepts:

- In order to determine whether a concept is androcentric, that is, has a referent restricted to males even though it presents itself as generally applicable to both sexes (e.g., "the suburb as a bedroom community," which conceptualizes the entire population of men, women, and children of the suburbs in terms of those individuals, originally primarily men, who leave in the morning to go to their paid work), "ask yourself the following questions: To whom or what does the concept appear to refer (who is the theoretical referent)? To whom or what does the concept *empirically* refer? Does it seem to refer to both sexes but empirically refer to one sex only? . . . If your answers to these questions indicate a mismatch between theoretical and empirical referents, the two must be made to match, either by changing the concept and making it sex-specific or by changing the content and making it applicable to both sexes" (Eichler 1988, 139–140 and see also 26).
- In order to determine whether a concept is "premised on a double standard," that is, "is based on an attribute that is potentially present in both sexes but is treated differently on the basis of sex" (as "head of household" or "head of family" is when used to refer to an adult married male, while an adult married female is referred to simply as "spouse," the attribute, here, being "is married"), "ask yourself the following question: Is the concept premised on an attribute that is present in both sexes but is operationally defined in such a manner that it will categorize females and males differently? . . . If you answered 'yes' to this question, you need to create a concept that categorizes females and males equally if they display equal attributes" (141–142 and see also 89–90).
- In order to determine whether a concept is "asymmetrical," that is, "describes a situation, trait, or behavior that is theoretically present in both sexes but is linked to one sex only" (as "unwed mother" is when not linked with "unwed father" or "maternal deprivation" is when not linked with "paternal deprivation"), "ask yourself the following question: Does the concept refer, in a sex-linked manner, to a situation, trait, or behavior that exists for both sexes? . . . If you answered 'yes' to this question, change the concept so that it expresses *human* attributes in sex-nonspecific terms" (142).

In all, Eichler's guidelines distinguished, illustrated, and offered recipes for eliminating seven different types of sexism in their most frequently occurring forms. Still, the guidelines made no pretense to being comprehensive. Indeed, Eichler's method for generating them was quite unsystematic: "My method was simple: I went into a library and picked up whatever recent issue of journals from different disciplines was lying on top in the journal pigeon holes. I assumed that it would make little difference which journal or issue I picked, and that I would find at least one example of sexism in every single one. Sadly, this turned out to be correct" (10).[2] In addition, Eichler's method relied on her perhaps limited knowledge of at least some of the scientific fields she covered, and as she herself pointed out, "the more trenchant critiques (and, one hopes, nonsexist alternatives) will have to emerge from within the various disciplinary groups" (132). Nevertheless, Eichler's guidelines were an important beginning.

Meanwhile, practitioners within the various disciplinary groups *were* offering their own more trenchant critiques and nonsexist alternatives. Feminist psychologist Carolyn Sherif, for example, suggested that "dominant beliefs about the proper way to pursue knowledge have made psychological research peculiarly prone to bias in its conception, execution and interpretation" (Sherif 1979, 63). These dominant beliefs included the view that psychology, in order to be truly scientific, should model its methods, concepts, and goals on those of the physical sciences—should, for example, emphasize physiological or biochemical variables and variables defined by performance on psychological tests or manipulation of circumstances in research situations. If it was to avoid the problem of bias, however, what psychology needed to do instead, urged Sherif, was to take account of such factors as the background, personal history, and gender of subjects and experimenters. It also needed to pursue research outside the laboratory or in naturalistic settings. In the past, for example, psychologists frequently reported that women were more suggestible or influenceable than men. But when psychologists started taking into account such factors as the gender of the researcher, the experimental context, and the interests and self-definition of subjects, their research results changed. They then found that women were more suggestible with a male researcher when the topic was socially defined as one of male interest, but also that men were more suggestible with a female researcher when the topic was socially defined as one of female interest. In short, failing to consider such factors as whether a topic was of concern to a subject and the gender of the researcher in relation to the topic had the effect of producing biased, spurious results of male/female difference and female inferiority within psychological research.

2. "The ease with which examples can be drawn from academic journals demonstrates the pervasiveness of sexism" (Eichler 1988, 9).

For their part, feminist biologists such as Ruth Bleier (1984), Evelyn Fox Keller (1983 and 1985), and Sue Rosser (1990) (see Longino 1994, 1995, 1997, and 2008) recommended that such traditionally central scientific values as consistency with established knowledge, simplicity, and explanatory unification be replaced by such alternative values as novelty, ontological heterogeneity, and complexity of relationship. The reason was that novelty, unlike the traditional consistency with established knowledge, would help to free science from a sexist and androcentric past. Ontological heterogeneity, unlike the traditional simplicity and explanatory unification, would help to make women's dissimilarities from men visible as signs not of women's inferiority to men, where men are taken as the sole norm or standard of comparison, but rather as signs of women's *differences* from men, where women and men have equal standing. And complexity of relationship, again unlike the traditional simplicity and explanatory unification, would help to steer theorizing away from simple dominant-subordinate conceptions of nature that naturalize social domination (as in older active-sperm-fertilizes-passive-egg models of fertilization) toward more complex interactive conceptions of nature (as in newer understandings of the interactive contributions to fertilization of both egg and sperm). Other feminist scientists called for still further discipline-specific as well as general methodological reforms for science.

THE IDEAL OF VALUE-FREE SCIENCE

A possible rationale for all of these reforms was provided by the ideal of value-free science—a possible rationale with impressive credentials. The ideal of value-free science, after all, was as old as modern science itself, and in its long and distinguished career it had garnered support from such varied sources as the seventeenth-century idea that nature is merely matter in motion, devoid of qualities such as good and evil; the eighteenth-century idea that science deals with facts and that facts are distinct from values; the nineteenth-century idea that the sciences should be impartial resources for the solution of social problems; and the twentieth-century idea that the establishment of scientific truths is a purely epistemic affair (see, for more details of this history, Proctor 1991). And the ideal of value-free science, in turn, supported just the right conclusion. According to value-free science, scientific investigations had to be kept strictly free of ethical or political commitments. Since sexism and androcentrism—whether in scientific concepts or data or methods or assumptions or hypotheses—embodied such commitments, they simply did not belong in science. Indeed, they biased science and thereby jeopardized science as a source of objective knowledge. Hence one of the tasks of an adequate scientific methodology properly applied was to screen out sexism and androcentrism (as well as racism and heterosexism), and when a methodology failed to do that, a reform of that methodology was called for. And this was precisely what feminist scientists pressing for more rigorous application of acceptable methodologies as well as methodological reforms were doing.

Of course, by the end of the twentieth century, the ideal of value-free science had fallen into disrepute. Mainstream historical scholarship had suggested that the work of even the greatest scientists—even scientists like Boyle and Darwin and Freud and even, perhaps, the great Newton and Einstein themselves—had been shaped by social values (see, e.g., Bernal 1971; Elkana 1982; Shapin and Schaffer 1985; Gilman 1993; Ruse 1999). If our conception of science, including our conception of objective science, was to be true to actual science, it could hardly ignore such science as this. Mainstream sociological research, in addition, had suggested that such value-informed science was all but inevitable. Indeed, any scientific contribution, we were told, was a product of a particular time and place, of a particular social and cultural location, of particular interests and values; a "view from nowhere," from a psychological and sociological vantage point, was simply naive (see, e.g., Knorr-Cetina 1981; Knorr-Cetina and Mulkay 1983; and Latour 1987). The ideal of value-free science, in short, seemed unlikely to be a viable ideal, useful for actual science. Mainstream philosophical analysis, finally, went one step further. It challenged the very distinction between social values and the scientific—the distinction between, for example, social values and economists' data about poverty or sociologists' and psychologists' measures of domestic abuse or archaeologists' accounts of human evolution and human flourishing or medical researchers' criteria of health and disease (see, e.g., Putnam 2002 and Dupré 2007). The ideal of value-free science, in short, according to this line of reasoning, might actually have been incoherent.

None of this necessarily tarnished the reputation of the ideal of value-free science among feminists, however. To begin with, none of it was especially new to feminists. Feminist scientists and historians and philosophers had already exposed sexism and androcentrism in even the greatest science (see, e.g., Merchant 1980 and Keller 1985 on early modern science; Hubbard 1979 on Darwin; and de Beauvoir [1949] 1972 and Horney 1950 on Freud), feminists had already regretfully acknowledged that such sexist science was to be expected from sexist societies, and feminists had already regretfully acknowledged how difficult it sometimes was to distinguish science from values, so permeated could science be, and sometimes was, with sexism. What's more, none of what mainstream historians and sociologists and philosophers of science had disclosed was especially damaging to the ideal of value-free science. If the greatest science was sexist, that did not mean that sexism in science was therefore acceptable. It simply meant that even the greatest science was not acceptable—not objective enough, simply not good enough. If sexist societies produced sexist science, science hardly distinguishable from mere prejudice, that did not mean that the ideal of value-free science was not useful for such societies but rather that it was extremely useful—and desperately needed—for precisely such societies. The ideal of value-free science, after all, offered hope that all could be made right—that science would be able, finally, to provide objective information about women and, in the process, expose and remove society's prejudice against women, not simply reinforce and perpetuate it. Thus, for example, feminist biologist Ruth Hubbard could admit that "There is no such thing as objective, value-free science. An era's science is part of its politics, economics and sociology: it is generated by them and in turn helps to generate them" (Hubbard 1979, 10) and quickly add that

> As scientists, we learn to examine the ways in which our experimental methods can bias our answers, but we are not taught to be equally wary of the biases introduced by our implicit, unstated and often unconscious beliefs about the nature of reality. To become conscious of these is more difficult than anything else we do. But difficult as it may seem, we must try to do it if our picture of the world is to be more than a reflection of various aspects of ourselves and of our social arrangements." (10–11)

And Hubbard could even go on to acknowledge in a footnote that although some "have characterized this process as 'trying to push a bus in which one is riding' . . . I would say that, worse yet, it is like trying to look out of the rear window to *watch* oneself push the bus in which one rides" (33, n. 2).

But the reputation of the ideal of value-free science *was* tarnished for feminists in a different way.[3] The work of feminist scientists clearly seemed more adequate and objective than the sexist and androcentric science it was designed to replace. That much was well documented by feminist historians of science such as Londa Schiebinger (1999). But it also seemed to be as shaped by feminist values as sexist science had been shaped by sexist values—for example, in the questions asked (think of Eichler) or the factors taken to be relevant when designing experiments (think of Sherif) or the factors taken to be relevant when constructing or evaluating hypotheses (think of Keller and Bleier and Rosser). And if feminists' science was shaped by feminist values, then according to the ideal of value-free science this should have made feminists' science just as subjective and inadequate as the sexist and androcentric science it was designed to replace. Feminist scientists struggled to respond. Some said that the function of feminist values in their research was purely motivational and not really a part of that research (Fausto-Sterling sometimes seemed to move in this direction; see, e.g., 1985, chapter 7). Others said that the function of feminist values in their research was not as a replacement for sexist values but as a new kind of methodological control to prevent the entry of sexist values into that research. "We have come to look at feminist critique

3. This was not the only reason feminists became disenchanted with the ideal of value-free science, of course. For example, some feminists argued that objectivity understood as value freedom was a masculinist conception, one that eschewed emotional attachment to the objects of knowledge and also discouraged women as knowers.

as we would any other experimental control," one widely quoted group of scientists said.

> Whenever one performs an experiment, one sets up all the controls one can think of in order to make as certain as possible that the result obtained does not come from any other source. One asks oneself what assumptions one is making. Have I assumed the temperature to be constant? Have I assumed that the pH doesn't change over the time of the reaction? Feminist critique asks if there may be some assumptions that we haven't checked concerning gender bias. In this way feminist critique should be part of normative science. Like any control, it seeks to provide critical rigor, and to ignore this critique is to ignore a possible source of error. (Biology and Gender Study Group 1988, 61–62; see also Eichler 1980, 118: "Feminist science is non-sexist" science)

Some even said that feminist science *was* after all just as subjective as sexist and androcentric science—that objectivity, in fact, was in principle impossible to achieve, by anyone (see, e.g., Stanley and Wise 1983). But in the end, feminist scientists concluded that a new and more adequate understanding of scientific objectivity was needed, one better equipped than the ideal of value-free science to deal with the problems of sexism and androcentrism in science and the scientific responses of feminists. Unfortunately, feminist scientists had few suggestions as to what that new understanding might be.[4]

Now, years later, feminist scientists are in scarcely better shape. True, a great deal of insightful work on the question of scientific objectivity has now been contributed by feminist philosophers of science, but no clear replacement for the ideal of value-free science has yet emerged. Promising candidates are available, of course, but as a group these candidates do not provide consistent advice to scientists or policy makers for ridding science of sexism and androcentrism (as well as racism, etc.) and sometimes even undercut one another. So a careful examination and comparison of their credentials is long overdue. Three of the most promising of these new understandings of scientific objectivity will be considered. Keep in mind the need for which this consideration is being carried out. The ideal of value-free science promised to play for feminist scientists both an epistemic role and a political role—promised to provide both a way to achieve objective knowledge and (by ridding science of sexism, androcentrism, and other inegalitarian values) a way to achieve social reform. And, of course, the two roles were connected, for

---

4. Feminist historian of science Elizabeth Fee was quoted approvingly when she emphasized the importance to an acceptable notion of scientific objectivity of "the willingness to consider all assumptions and methods as open to question and the expectation that ideas will be subjected to the most unfettered critical evaluation" (1983, 16); Eichler added "a commitment to 'truth-finding'" and "a clarification and classification of values underlying the research" (1988, 14); Bleier (1984, 204) added "critical self-reflection" ("a part of this process is recognizing the degree to which investment of ego and pride in one's previously stated beliefs and theories may corrupt the scientific approach"); and so on. But that's about as far as the discussion got.

the epistemic role was to make possible the political role; objective knowledge was to make possible social reform. Any acceptable replacement for the ideal of value-free science will have to play these two roles as well.

THE SOCIAL VALUE MANAGEMENT IDEAL OF SCIENCE: A SOCIAL APPROACH TO SEXISM IN SCIENCE

Doubtless the most well known of the candidates available to take the place of the ideal of value-free science is the one put forward by feminist philosopher of science Helen Longino (see, for what follows, Longino 1990 and 2002). It relies, to begin with, on a disambiguation of the notion of scientific objectivity. "Science is thought to provide us with a view of the world that is objective in two seemingly quite different senses of that term" (Longino 1990, 62). In one sense, scientific objectivity has to do with the truth of scientific claims to knowledge. In the second sense, scientific objectivity has to do with the distinctive procedures scientists use to obtain that knowledge—what philosophers of science have called scientific rationality. "Common wisdom has it that if science is objective in the first sense it is because it is objective in the second" (63). So the key to the more adequate understanding of scientific objectivity sought by feminist scientists of the past is a more adequate understanding of scientific rationality. And for Longino, that will be a social understanding.

Indeed, the problem, according to Longino, is that feminist scientists of the past focused on the scientific methods of individual scientists to screen out of science social values such as sexism and androcentrism. But no scientific methods, however rigorous and however rigorously applied, can be guaranteed to screen out the various values and interests that scientists bring to their research. To be sure, scientists' values and interests can and do determine which questions they investigate and which they ignore, can and do motivate the background assumptions they accept and those they reject, can and do influence the observational or experimental data they select to study and the way they interpret those data, and so on. The ideal appropriate for science, Longino thus suggests, is not the ideal of value-free science but the "social value management" (Longino 2002, 50) ideal of science. According to this ideal, all social values should be welcomed into science—indeed, encouraged—and all social values, and the science they engender, should be subjected to criticism. So there is a kind of neutrality here, akin to the ideal of value-free science. The only restrictions, in fact, have to do with the social organization of scientific communities. These communities, Longino insists, will have to have, first, public venues for criticism, such as journals and conferences; second, publicly recognized standards—substantive principles as well as values—by reference to which the criticism can be made; third, "uptake" of the criticism (i.e., the beliefs of the scientific community as a whole and over time, as measured by such public phenomena as the content of textbooks, the distribution of grants and awards, and the flexibility of dominant world views, will have to change in response to the critical discussion taking place within it); and fourth, "tempered equality" of intellectual authority among all parties to the debate, among whom "all relevant perspectives [that can serve as sources of criticism] are represented" (Longino 2002, 131). A science will, then, be *objective—rational*—to the degree that it satisfies these four conditions, to the degree that it permits what Longino calls "transformative criticism" (1990, 76). And the output of such a science will constitute *knowledge*, even if that output is inspired and informed by social values, if the community that practices it meets these conditions and the output conforms sufficiently to its objects to enable the members of the community to carry out their projects with respect to those objects.

Thus, for Longino's social value management ideal of science, scientific rationality ("objectivity") is a function of the workings of scientific communities, not—as with the ideal of value-free science and the more formal methodological approach it rationalizes—the attitudes and behavior of individual scientists.[5] Will this new ideal with its social approach prove more successful than the old ideal with its methodological approach in dealing with sexism and androcentrism in science in a defensible way? What credentials assure us that it will? In her book *The Fate of Knowledge* (2002), Longino does much to exhibit these credentials. She shows her social value management ideal of science informed by some of the most important findings of sociohistorical research. She shows her ideal informed, as well, by the enduring insights of epistemological reflection. At the same time, she shows her ideal able to integrate all of these findings and insights into a coherent account of science, an account free of the confusions that have frequently accompanied them. Most important, however, Longino implies that her ideal embodies just what we have been looking for to replace the ideal of value-free science, just what we mean by terms such as *knowledge* and *rationality*. Granted, this last accolade somewhat strains credulity. After all, all of us, before Longino wrote, thought we had some handle on the meanings of these terms, but doubtless most of us had no handle on what Longino describes, tempered equality and public venues and uptake and the rest, not even a preanalytic, prearticulated version of what she describes.[6] No matter. If Longino's candidate is

---

5. This is the point that most clearly distinguishes Longino's approach from that of the feminist scientists mentioned in note 4 above.

6. Certainly, the sorts of questions Longino says must be answered in order to complete her analysis—for example, "In determining what counts as inappropriate exclusion of dissenting perspectives, does it matter what kind of issue is involved?" and "What bearing should greater cognitive authority have on the attribution of intellectual authority, understood as the capacity to participate in critical discussion and thus to contribute to critical understanding?" (Longino 2002, 133)—certainly these sorts of questions do not seem answerable by yet another round of reflection on the meaning of *knowledge* and related terms.

most comfortable in the dress of traditional analytic philosophy, then it is in the dress of traditional analytic philosophy that it shall be given its examination.

On, then, to the imaginary tale, de rigueur in traditional epistemology. But this time, the tale is not about some solitary epistemic agent named Smith, his lucky happenstances, and his (usually unsuccessful) claims to knowledge, as in days of old, but about a scientific *community* named Smith—or, rather, named PETERS, that is, the Privileged, Exclusive, Talented, Elite, Royal Society. PETERS is made up of a subset of the privileged and talented of society S, but PETERS is also a very elite society, very exclusive. It excludes all those, albeit sometimes talented, persons who fall into various unfavored classes (the nonprivileged, the underprivileged). And PETERS has power—it is, after all, a royal society. So PETERS, knowing where its bread is buttered and also sharing in the perspectives of the butterers, pursues a particular kind of cognitive enterprise, one that serves its particular needs and interests. PETERS, of course, is a scientific society, concerned with understanding the world and interacting with it successfully. But PETERS is also a privileged, exclusive, talented, elite, royal scientific society, and that leaves a definite mark on the parts of the world it seeks to understand and the ways it seeks to interact with them. So, for example, PETERS investigates physical and chemical questions related to its concern with war making and military preeminence, PETERS investigates biological and psychological questions related to its concern with the maladies that afflict the privileged and the reasons they are superior nonetheless, PETERS investigates archaeological questions related to its concern with the routes by which the privileged have achieved their superior state of development, and so forth. And PETERS's concepts and theories and models and methods and standards and values reflect these concerns, these privilegecentric and privilegist goals.

Our question is, would PETERS, over time, produce *knowledge* for its members? We can imagine that PETERS regularly holds conferences and publishes journals in which all its members are encouraged to participate and in which all are treated equally. We can imagine that in these venues, prolonged and frequently heated critical exchanges take place, exchanges that pay scrupulous attention to shared standards. We can imagine that follow-up exchanges regularly take place as well. And we can imagine that the intellectual products that emerge from all of this activity conform well enough to their objects to enable PETERS to pursue its (privilegecentric and privilegist) projects to its (or, rather, its members') satisfaction. We can even imagine that, after some time, PETERS invites, even encourages, members of the underprivileged classes—at least, their talented members— to join its ranks, master its methods and standards and values and concepts and models and theories, and contribute to its (privilegecentric and privilegist) projects; we can even imagine that PETERS encourages these underprivileged ones to develop "alternative points of view" that can serve as a "source of criticism and new perspectives" (see Longino 2002, 132), so that finally "all relevant perspectives are represented" (see Longino 2002, 131) in PETERS's exchanges, that is to say, all perspectives relevant to the satisfaction of PETERS's privilegecentric and privilegist goals. Would PETERS now be producing knowledge for its members? It would seem that Longino's candidate must answer yes, although it should answer no. And would that knowledge—if it is knowledge—be free of privilegecentric and privilegist prejudices and thereby a suitable springboard from which to bring about social reform in society S rather than a reinforcement of those same prejudices? It would seem that we must answer no.

"Stop the examination," I hear you saying. "It's unfair! It's rigged! Longino's candidate is getting pushed in a direction it does not want to go. When Longino says that in order for a scientific community's critical interactions to generate knowledge, 'all relevant perspectives' must be represented, she does not only mean all perspectives that might serve that community's goals; she means all perspectives that might relate in any way at all to those goals, that is to say, all perspectives that might support them, or clarify them, or develop them, or add to them, or revise them, or replace them, and so on. 'Such criticism,' she says, 'may originate from an indeterminate number of points of view, none of which may be excluded from the community's interactions without cognitive impairment'" (Longino 2002, 133).

OK. Start the examination again. Imagine once again that PETERS finally encourages members of the underprivileged classes to join its ranks and develop alternative points of view—all relevant alternative points of view—that can serve as sources of criticism and new perspectives. Would PETERS now be producing knowledge for its members? And would that knowledge—if it is knowledge—be free of privilegecentric and privilegist prejudices and thereby a suitable springboard from which to bring about social reform in society S? We cannot now say simply that PETERS's cognitive output would have to serve its original privilegecentric and privilegist goals and thereby serve the status quo in society S, for over time PETERS's cognitive output might evolve in all sorts of ways as a result of the critical discourse occurring in it. The underprivileged ones in PETERS, though trained in its privilegecentric and privilegist research traditions, might come to have the wherewithal to develop alternatives to some of those traditions, perhaps aided by changes over time in PETERS or in PETERS's science or in PETERS's surrounding society S. The underprivileged ones in PETERS might even succeed over time in building significant support for some of these alternatives, might even succeed in crystallizing new research traditions around some of them that parallel in many ways the older traditions, might even bring about the replacement of some of the older traditions. Women, after all, originally largely excluded from Western science and then, when included, trained in its androcentric and sexist research traditions, still came to have the wherewithal to develop alternatives to some of those traditions, aided by the sheer numbers of women—the "critical mass" of women—in some research areas, and aided by the women's movement in society at large as well as by changes in other academic fields. Women even succeeded over time in building support for some of these alternatives, even succeeded in crystallizing new feminist research programs around some of them to compete with the older programs, even succeeded in replacing some of the older programs. The underprivileged ones in PETERS, though trained in its privilegecentric and privilegist research traditions, then, might come to have the wherewithal to replace them. But then again, they might not. They might not have egalitarian political movements in society S to aid them, they might have political backlash instead; they might be stymied by available mathematical resources or instrumental technologies or preferred modes of analysis; they might be affected by funding cutbacks or staffing problems or family needs. Certainly, women in science have been thwarted by such factors as these, and certainly, women in science have met with far less than unbridled success in trying to rid science of sexism and androcentrism.

So, what is the upshot? If what PETERS produces is *knowledge* for its members according to Longino's social value management ideal of science, this knowledge need not be free of privilegecentric and privilegist prejudices,[7] need not be a suitable springboard from which to bring about social reform in society S. If Longino's ideal fulfills the epistemic role of the old ideal of value-free science, in short, it still may not fulfill the political role.[8] Well, so what? Had the ideal of value-free science been acceptable, it would have provided a way to rid science of sexist and androcentric values and the like and thereby promote social equality. But the ideal of value-free science was *not* acceptable. So why should its successor have actually to do what it, itself, merely promised but could not actually do? Why, in short, should the successor of the ideal of value-free science have to play a political role along with an epistemic role? Then again, if we excuse the successor of the ideal of value-free science from playing its predecessor's political role, we not only lose scientific knowledge as an ally in the fight for social justice, we set scientific knowledge up as part of the problem, part of what reinforces and perpetuates prejudice rather than exposes and removes it. Is there a better way to go?

7. This may be a reason to deny that what PETERS produces is knowledge after all—that is, to deny that Longino's social value management ideal of science fulfills the epistemic role of the old ideal of value-free science.

8. Of course, Longino might say at this point that if the requisite political movements or analytic methods or mathematical resources or instrumental technologies or funding or staffing or family supports were not there to aid the underprivileged ones in PETERS, then "all relevant perspectives" were not there in PETERS, either. Hence the conclusion to be drawn is not that the social value management ideal of science fails to fulfill the political role of the old ideal of value-free science but that the social value management ideal of science has not been provided with a genuine test case to see if it does. But such a response on Longino's part would threaten to make her candidate's fulfillment of the political role of the ideal of value-free science true by definition (of "all relevant perspectives are represented"). It would also threaten to make her candidate unrealizable in practice—just the sort of problem that caused the need to replace the ideal of value-free science to begin with.

THE EMPIRICIST IDEAL OF SCIENCE: A NATURALIST APPROACH TO SEXISM IN SCIENCE

Consider a second candidate, put forward by feminist philosophers of a more naturalist bent than Longino. This candidate—call it the empiricist ideal of science—rejects a priori prescriptions regarding the proper composition of scientific communities or the proper conduct of inquiry. It rejects, as well, the single-minded focus of its predecessor on scientific practice to the exclusion of scientific outcome. What the empiricist ideal advocates, instead, is a close look at *successful* scientific practice in order to identify those of its features that contribute to and explain its success. For the empiricist ideal, in fact, scientific rationality just *is* whatever contributes to and explains scientific success (see, e.g., Antony 1993, 1995; Solomon 2001). Can the empiricist ideal, with this understanding of scientific rationality, fulfill the political as well as epistemic roles of the old ideal of value-free science? What reasons suggest that it can?

When we take a close look at successful scientific practice during the last three decades, we find that a great deal of that part of it that is gender-relevant has been produced by feminists. We find, that is to say, that the contributions of feminists—the wide-ranging critiques of traditional science in such fields as psychology, sociology, economics, political science, archaeology, anthropology, biology, and medical research and the new research directions and research results forged in the wake of those critiques—these contributions have been not only free of sexism and androcentrism but also more empirically successful than the sexist and androcentric science that went before (see, e.g., Schiebinger 1999 and Creager, Lunbeck, and Schiebinger 2001 for the kinds of wide-ranging changes in science that have occurred due to feminism). What features of this successful science explain its success? There are at least two possibilities, both offered by feminist naturalists. The first—the standpoint hypothesis—suggests that the success of feminists' science may be due in large part to the fact that feminists tend to be women and women, other things being equal, tend to be in a better position than men to detect sexism and androcentrism in science and replace them with more adequate perspectives. After all, feminist philosopher of science Sandra Harding reminds us, sexism and androcentrism directly benefit men, whereas they oppress women. As a consequence, women in general—and women scientists in particular—are more likely than their male counterparts to be critical of such values. "They have less to lose by distancing themselves from the social order; thus, the perspective from their lives can more easily generate fresh and critical analyses" (Harding 1991, 126; see also Wylie 2003 and 2007, which treat standpoint theory more explicitly as a naturalist hypothesis). The second—the values hypothesis—suggests that the success of feminists' science may be less a function of feminists' standpoints than of feminists' values, where values, like any other apparently nonepistemic feature of scientific practice (such as competitiveness or the desire for credit for one's accomplishments), need not function as hindrances but might actually function as aids in the acquisition of objective knowledge. Indeed, supporters of this second hypothesis point out that cases in which feminist values have clearly influenced science (e.g., by motivating particular lines of research or the maintenance of particular social structures) *have* been cases in which the science produced is not only free of sexism but also more developed and more empirically adequate than before (see, e.g., Antony 1993, 1995; Campbell 2001; Anderson 1995, 2004; Wylie and Nelson 2007). Now, if either of these hypotheses is correct—that is to say, if feminists through the one means (standpoints) or the other (values) *produce* scientific success, more scientific success than sexists—then, of course, the scientific ideal that defines rationality in terms of the production of scientific success will thereby guarantee that feminist science is rational science (i.e., more rational science), and sexist science is not (is less). If either of these (feminist naturalists') hypotheses is correct, in short, then the empiricist ideal of science *will* fulfill the political as well as epistemic roles of the old ideal of value-free science.

So runs the empiricist ideal's defense. It hinges, of course, on the correctness of at least one of the above feminist naturalist hypotheses. But is either one of these hypotheses correct? Consider, to begin with, the standpoint hypothesis. What kind of evidence do we have in its favor? Certainly, women scientists have achieved breakthroughs that the men scientists before them did not, breakthroughs that seemed clearly connected to the fact that they were made by women. For example, biological anthropologist Sarah Blaffer Hrdy reports that, in the face of abundant, generally available evidence to the contrary, modern sexual selection theory up to the mid-1970s still featured sexually aggressive, promiscuous males actively courting sexually "coy," passive females. Males were very much the focus of investigation, and such topics as female promiscuity and the effect of female social status and female expertise in child-rearing on female reproductive success were ignored. With the significant influx of women into primatology starting in the 1970s, however, all that changed. The women brought with them new, nonandrocentric, nonsexist perceptions and questions and hypotheses about female primates. And the result for primatology, says Hrdy, has been a new focus on female reproductive strategies and, with it, a fundamental rethinking of sexual selection theory (Hrdy 1986). Again, in her 1971 study of 30 impoverished black teenage girls, sociologist Joyce Ladner explains that because she was a black woman, with a black woman's socialization and life experiences—in effect, a black woman's perspective—she found herself dealing with her black female subjects' problems on a personal level as well as on a professional level, in terms of the sociological concepts ("social deviance," "social disorganization," "social pathology," etc.) she had been taught. And what came out of this "double consciousness" was not only a quite radical reconceptualization of the girls' pregnancy, school dropout, and other problems ("a very healthy and successful adaptation, given their limited resources, had been made by all of these girls to a set of very unhealthy environmental conditions") but also a quite radical reconceptualization of significant parts of sociological theory and methodology (Ladner 1971).

Certainly, then, women scientists have achieved breakthroughs that men scientists have not, breakthroughs that seemed closely connected to the fact that they were made by women. But women scientists have also made contributions indistinguishable from those of the men, contributions sometimes just as sexist and androcentric as those of the men. For example, a December 2006 study analyzing 40 years of gender-difference research published in four journals of the American Psychological Association (a broader range of journals was also studied in less depth, to assess representativeness of the findings) showed that males are still treated as the norm in this research against which girls and women are measured. The striking point to be noted here is that between 1965 and 2004, the years covered in the study, the journals studied ceased to be male-dominated: roughly equal numbers of females and males were represented among both the published authors and the research subjects. In short, this new study shows that women psychologists' research regarding gender differences continues to be just as androcentric as men's (and also that men's research is sometimes just as free of sexism and androcentrism as women's—the study authors, after all, are a man and a woman) (Hegarty and Buechel 2006). But there are also plenty of more familiar examples to the same effect: the originator and most militant promoter of the idea of premenstrual syndrome (PMS) was a woman physician and researcher, Katharina Dalton; the scientists who seek to explain greater male than female aggressiveness in terms of prenatal hormone exposure include many prominent women researchers (e.g., Anke Ehrhardt and June Reinisch); the scientists who seek to explain the differences in women's and men's status in society in terms of biologically based cognitive differences include many prominent women researchers (e.g., Sandra Witelson and Doreen Kimura), and so on (see, for more details, Fausto-Sterling 1985).

Of course, few standpoint theorists extend an automatic epistemic/political advantage to women scientists. The women's standpoint they speak of must be discovered and developed through a collective process of political struggle—through some sort of feminist consciousness raising and solidarity building. Even Alison Wylie, who has presented survey evidence to show that it was women archaeologists' standpoint as women, not their feminist consciousness (which half the time they denied having), that brought about the dramatic changes in archaeology that began in the late 1980s (Wylie 1997)—even Alison Wylie has qualified this claim. In "Doing Social Science as a Feminist: The Engendering of Archeology," for example, she speaks of "feminist commitments and insights" as having played "a critical, if often indirect, role" in producing the changes (Wylie 2001, 28). And Sarah Hrdy also points to the influence of feminism to explain how women primatologists were able to bring about a fundamental rethinking of sexual selection theory in the 1970s and 1980s. Indeed, she speculates that women primatologists identified with primates of their own sex, just as the men primatologists had done before them, and allowed this identification to influence their research focus. But because feminism was then changing the self-perception of these women, their identification with female primates was simultaneously leading them to their new nonandrocentric, nonsexist perceptions and questions and hypotheses about female primates. Some such feminist consciousness is necessary, according to standpoint theorists, in order to achieve the relevant standpoint, the sort of standpoint that leads to more adequate, nonsexist science. And perhaps it is this feminist consciousness that is lacking in the cases in which the contributions of women scientists are just as inadequate and sexist as those of their male counterparts. But exactly what kind of feminist consciousness is necessary is never specified, certainly not clearly enough to allow the standpoint hypothesis to be put to a reasonable test. And to the extent that a feminist consciousness is held to be crucial, to that extent the standpoint hypothesis starts metamorphosing into the values hypothesis.

Of course, the values hypothesis has problems of its own. Even in the case of the so-called feminist contributions to science over the last three decades, its advocates would be hard pressed to show that the progress that was made in every case was the effect of feminist values rather than other factors. Sometimes, in fact, the point is acknowledged by those reflecting on that progress. For example, the Biology and Gender Study Group claims only that the eye-opening studies that led to new models of fertilization and sex determination in the 1980s "can be viewed as feminist-influenced critiques of cell and molecular biology": "It should be noted that the views expressed in this essay may or may not be those of the scientists whose work we have reviewed. It is our contention that these research programs are inherently critical of a masculinist assumption with these respective fields. This does not mean that the research was consciously done with this in mind" (Biology and Gender Study Group 1988, 68, 74, n. 5). The values hypothesis has deeper problems than the solidity of its evidence, however. After all, it treats feminists' egalitarian values as merely causally relevant "social factors" or "social biases," on a par with other factors such as competitiveness or the desire for credit or other values such as sexism or racism.[9] All of these become possible aids to the

---

9. Antony (1993) and Campbell (2001) classify together sexism and racism along with feminist social values as "biases." They then make a distinction between "good biases" (those that "facilitate the gathering of knowledge," that is, those that "lead us to the truth") and "bad biases" (those that "lead us away from the truth"). In short, *we must treat the goodness or badness of particular biases as an empirical question*" (Antony 1993 215, emphasis hers; and see Campbell 2001, 196, who quotes Antony approvingly, although he tries for a more elaborate kind of naturalism in Campbell 1998). Solomon (2001) also classifies together sexism, racism, and egalitarian social values, now as "ideology," and goes on to classify together these ideological social factors ("decision vectors" or causes for theory choice) with other "non-empirical" decision vectors such as birth order, desire for credit, deference to authority, and competitiveness. But, for her, an equal distribution of such nonempirical decision vectors among competing theories is what generally helps to produce "normatively appropriate" science.

production of scientific success, and all must be empirically tested to see if they are. Any of them will do, we are led to infer, if only they can prove their mettle in scientific research. (This is made explicit when "good" social values in science are *defined* as those that aid the acquisition of objective knowledge, those that are epistemically fruitful.) So if, for example, a close comparative study of German medical science before, during, and after the Third Reich discloses that Nazi social values produced the best scientific results, the most abundant and most empirically successful science, then Nazi social values would be good values and should therefore be welcomed into science. Or if such a study discloses that Nazi social values produced a science just as successful as the others but no better, then it should be a matter of complete indifference whether Nazi social values or the other sciences' values should find their way into science, since none of the values would be justified over the others. And this is remarkable given that one of the main factors that brought about the success of Nazi medical science was the absence in it of good social values—for example, the absence (sanctioned by Nazi social values) of moral constraints on human experimentation.

This is not to say that the epistemic success (or failure) of a scientific research project tells us nothing about the justifiability of the social values that guide it. But what it tells us must take into account a great many other factors besides that outcome—for example, which scientists were involved in the project, the level of their talents and training, and the conceptual, material, and social resources at their disposal. Factors such as these help to explain the failure of research guided by arguably good social values (such as some of the egalitarian social values guiding Lysenko) and also help to explain the success of research guided by clearly bad social values (such as the racist social values guiding the Nazis). But, of course, moral and legal principles, as well, are relevant to the assessment of the social values that guide scientific research—think of the respect for individual autonomy and self-determination and the Hippocratic Oath's admonition that physicians should "abstain from all intentional wrongdoing and harm" that informed the response to Nazi medical research in the Nuremberg Doctors Trial and the Nuremberg Code on human experimentation that followed (Katz 1996). And these moral and legal principles, in turn, are themselves informed by factual considerations, including the factual considerations that result from scientific inquiry. What all of this shows is that the assessment of the social values that guide a scientific research project, whatever the epistemic outcome of that project, is a complex, multifaceted undertaking.

The upshot is that the hypotheses underwriting the empiricist ideal's defense—the values hypothesis no less than the standpoint hypothesis—are just that, hypotheses, and quite problematic hypotheses at that. They show at most that the empiricist ideal *may* be able to fulfill the epistemic and political roles of the old ideal of value-free science; they give us no strong reasons for thinking that the empiricist ideal *will* be able actually

68

Philosophy of Science after Feminism

to do so. This is, unfortunately, the same sort of conclusion we came to when we considered Longino's proposed social value management ideal of science. There, again, we found that her ideal may be able to fulfill the political as well as epistemic roles of the old ideal of value-free science, but we were left with no strong reasons for thinking that it would actually do so. If we are to pin our hopes for a science that is at once truly rational and truly a basis for social reform on a new understanding of scientific rationality (objectivity), we need a stronger candidate for that understanding than these.

THE IDEAL OF SOCIALLY RESPONSIBLE SCIENCE: A POLITICAL APPROACH TO SEXISM IN SCIENCE

There is, however, one more candidate awaiting examination—a less sophisticated candidate, by far, than the others but with a certain down-to-earth, home-spun charm. It can be called the ideal of socially responsible science. Coming after the other candidates, as it is, this candidate has had the opportunity to learn from their insights as well as their mistakes. Thus, like the ideal of value-free science, the ideal of socially responsible science recognizes that sexism and androcentrism must be rooted out of science if science is to replace prevailing ignorance and prejudice and misinformation about women with more adequate perspectives, but unlike the ideal of value-free science, the ideal of socially responsible science also recognizes that rooting sexism and androcentrism out of science is tantamount to implanting egalitarian social values into science. Like the social value management ideal of science, on the other hand, the ideal of socially responsible science recognizes that social values inevitably enter into science, but unlike the social value management ideal of science, the ideal of socially responsible science also recognizes that we, as a society, have a definite say—through funding priorities and restrictions, for example—as to what these social values will be. Indeed, given that science is both a profound shaper of society and a profound beneficiary of society, these social values should be chosen so as to meet the needs of society, including the justice-related needs of society. And finally, like the empiricist ideal of science, the ideal of socially responsible science recognizes that scientific rationality must be defined in terms of scientific success, but unlike the empiricist ideal of science, the ideal of socially responsible science also recognizes that scientific success must be defined in terms of social success—human flourishing, what makes for a good society—as well as empirical success. Under the ideal of socially responsible science, in short, our scientific views—and hence, ultimately, our generally accepted knowledge—would no longer be plagued by sexism and androcentrism (as well as racism and other inegalitarian values) simply because those would be the morally justified political conditions under which scientific research would be pursued.

The ideal of socially responsible science is thus able to fulfill the political role of the old ideal of value-free science. But is it able to fulfill the political role by safeguarding science as a genuine source of knowledge—as the ideal of value-free science aspired to do—or is it able to fulfill the political role by sacrificing science as a genuine source of knowledge? In short, is the ideal of socially responsible science able to fulfill the epistemic role as well as the political role of the ideal of value-free science? This is the question we need answered if we are to determine whether the ideal of socially responsible science can fill the position now vacated by the ideal of value-free science. Since the ideal of socially responsible science seems to be the ideal to which many feminist scientists now subscribe, it will be helpful to examine it in the context of what these scientists are actually doing. A positive outcome of the examination will then provide not only a rationale for what these scientists are doing but also a very concrete model of what other scientists can and ought to do. And a negative outcome will provide an equally concrete model and rationale for what these and other scientists ought not to do.

Consider, then, a new psychological research program described by Carolyn West, concerned with the problem of domestic violence in the United States (West 2002; and see West 2004). The aim of this program is complex: to uncover the similarities in intimate-partner violence within the black and white communities of the United States without negating the experiences of black women and simultaneously to highlight the differences within the black and white communities without perpetuating the stereotype that black Americans are inherently more violent than other ethnic groups. This aim requires charting a new course for research. For example, it requires broadening the definition of partner violence to include psychological, emotional, verbal, and sexual abuse as well as physical abuse. It also requires changing the ways violence is measured—from merely counting violent acts and measuring their severity (which focuses on discrete male behaviors) to taking into account the contexts, motives, and outcomes of the violent acts (which focuses on female experiences) using a combination of qualitative and quantitative research methods, including listening to the voices of battered women. All this dramatically transforms the picture of racial similarities and differences drawn from past research—the picture according to which, for example, black women, when compared with their white counterparts, are significantly more likely to sustain and inflict aggression, especially aggression involving weapons and culminating in hospitalization. The new research program involves other changes as well, such as a revision of measurement scales to reflect more than the experiences of white European Americans taken as the norm and investigations of within-group differences in the black and white communities to determine whether what appear to be racial differences are not simply socioeconomic differences instead. And the program involves integrating participants into every stage of the research process, from planning to implementing, interpreting, and disseminating results, in order to reduce one-sided research interpretations. The result is the kind of research that both motivates social reform and helps to bring it about.

Our question is, what are the effects of the egalitarian social values that operate within West's research program? Do they compromise the justifiability of the knowledge the program provides? First, what are these values? They seem to be "Women deserve to live without fear of violence from domestic partners" and "Black women deserve the same opportunities as white women to live in such partnerships." These values are well justified both inside and outside feminist theory; they should be uncontroversial. Second, what role do these values play in the program? Remember that West makes it a central part of her aim not to perpetuate the stereotype that black Americans are inherently more violent than other ethnic groups. The reason is that this stereotype in people's minds—in the minds of researchers and politicians and service providers, for example—makes it more likely that black women's needs related to domestic violence will be treated less seriously than white women's needs, or even ignored altogether. After all, if violence is perceived as inevitable—as somehow innate or unique to the black culture—intervention efforts are more likely to be perceived as futile. In short, if black women deserve the same opportunities as white women to live in domestic partnerships free of violence—West's egalitarian social value—then the stereotype connecting blacks and violence must not be perpetuated. This means that West's research program, as far as empirically possible, must highlight the similarities in domestic violence within the black and white communities and seek to explain whatever dissimilarities appear within these communities in terms of social differences such as racism and poverty.[10] But none of this must obscure in any way black women's experiences, since to do so would again be to shortchange black women's needs and, hence, fail to provide black women the same opportunities as white women to live in partnerships free of violence.

The upshot: West's research program is controlled through and through by sound egalitarian social values. But it is equally controlled through and through by sound epistemic values. Although the science here is thoroughly politicized, in short, it is not at the expense of its mission to provide

---

10. One example West presents:

Black feminist thought can make a significant contribution by keeping the focus on historical perspectives. During slavery and well into reconstruction, Black women witnessed their husbands, fathers, sons, and brothers being abducted by slave owners, police officers, and Klansmen. For the contemporary Black woman, having her partner arrested may be reminiscent of these earlier historical traumas. Although she wants the violence to stop, she may be reluctant to thrust her batterer into a system that is discriminatory, hostile, and overcrowded with Black males. Batterers realize this and will often use this history to further manipulate their partners. Black feminists recommend that this history be acknowledged while simultaneously holding African-American men accountable for their abuse. (2002, 229)

genuine knowledge. And this should not be the least bit surprising. After all, research such as West's cannot fulfill its social objectives, cannot effect improvements for battered women in both the black and white communities, unless it does fulfill its epistemic objectives, unless it does get a firm handle on the reality it means to reform. But this means that research such as West's, with its two kinds of interrelated objectives, social and epistemic, shaped by two kinds of values, social and epistemic, should be judged by two kinds of standards, not one—by moral/political standards as well as by epistemic standards. Such research should be found wanting if it fails sound epistemic requirements. But it should also be found wanting if it is shaped by unacceptable social values. How else can science take its rightful place in the forefront of social change?

WHERE YOU TAKE OVER THE EXAMINATION OF THE IDEAL OF SOCIALLY RESPONSIBLE SCIENCE

So, do the egalitarian social values that operate within West's research program compromise the justifiability of the knowledge the program provides? They do not. The candidate has successfully answered our question.

"Not at all," you exclaim, voice rising. "The answer given is too quick. Indeed, the answer given makes it look as though the epistemic objectives and the social objectives of a research program such as West's can never conflict, so that the social objectives, or the social values that lie behind them, can never contaminate the knowledge produced. But this is far too optimistic. After all, what if the stereotype that black Americans are inherently more violent than other ethnic groups were true?[11] The egalitarian-value-directed research program described would never allow this truth to be discovered, and the ideal of socially responsible science would never allow any less egalitarian research program to be pursued—say, one that straightforwardly investigated the truth of the stereotype by searching for cultural factors associated with violence, cultural factors that differ from one ethnic group to another. So, in this case, social objectives and epistemic objectives would clearly conflict, and the ideal of socially responsible science would sacrifice the epistemic objectives for the sake of the social. This means that the ideal of socially responsible science cannot

---

11. Note that West begins by explaining that the studies conducted to date present a "contradictory" picture of racial differences in domestic violence. "In summary, some researchers found similar rates of partner violence across racial groups. . . . In contrast, other investigators discovered that Black women, when compared to their White counterparts, were significantly more likely to sustain and inflict aggression. Moreover, they were more likely to be victims of severe violence. This pattern was reported at every stage on the relationship continuum" (2002, 218). West's research program is a socially and epistemically sophisticated way to deal with this contradictory situation. What is now being suggested is that there may be other ways, and perhaps even better ways, to deal with it that should also be considered.

be relied on to fulfill the epistemic role as well as the political role of the old ideal of value-free science."

"Not so," comes the candidate's reply. (This candidate is not about to concede defeat!) "If the stereotype connecting blacks and violence were true, that truth *could* be discovered with West's program. All the program requires, remember, is that dissimilarities in domestic violence within the black and white communities be explained, *as far as empirically possible*, in terms of social differences such as racism and poverty. The program does not guarantee that any of these explanations will be successful. Indeed, if the stereotype connecting blacks and violence were true, all of these explanations at best would have limited success (depending on whether they also were true), and that would provide (indirect) support for the stereotype. And since a central aim of the program is to make black women's experiences with domestic violence as visible as white women's experiences, the dissimilarities between the two would be made visible as well—just those dissimilarities whose failure to be socially explained would count in favor of the stereotype. So neither the ideal of socially responsible science nor West's particular research program sanctioned by that ideal makes knowledge unreachable. Nor do they 'contaminate' the knowledge produced. They simply channel science's search for knowledge in some directions and away from others in response to the needs we present as a society."[12]

"But the 'channeling' runs very deep!" you retort, irritation in your voice. "It affects not only research questions but also, as we have seen, such aspects of research as concepts (e.g., the concept of 'partner violence' itself); measurement scales and techniques; methods of subject selection; strategies of data collection, analysis, and interpretation; and even methods of publishing and disseminating results. It may even affect other central

12. We can think of West's program as a Lakatosian research program (see Lakatos 1970). Her denial of the stereotype that black Americans are inherently more violent than other ethnic groups is part of the "hard core" of the program. Her instructions to highlight similarities and to explain away dissimilarities between the black and white communities are part of the "negative heuristic" of the program that protects the hard core from refutation. And her instructions regarding how to do this—for example, to revise concepts such as "partner violence" to uncover similarities and to formulate hypotheses to explain dissimilarities in terms of social factors such as racism and poverty—are part of the "positive heuristic" of the program. Finally, although Lakatos never considered social values as playing a legitimate role within scientific research programs, what motivates West's program are her egalitarian social values. What the candidate has just been saying is that there are conditions under which it will be rational to abandon (to consider "refuted") West's research program, conditions that Lakatos tried to describe in detail. Notice, however, that the abandonment of West's research program would not necessarily justify the abandonment ("refutation") of West's egalitarian social values, for reasons that were made clear above. For example, if it were concluded that the stereotype about black Americans is true (which is the denial of the program's hard core), say, because violence is inherent in black culture, it would not follow that black women do not deserve the same opportunities as white women to live without fear of violence from domestic partners. See, for example, the complicated debate about the relationship between feminism and multiculturalism in Okin 1999.

aspects of the research process, such as consideration of the consequences of error and setting acceptable levels of risk (see, e.g., Douglas 2000). So the ideal of socially responsible science and the research programs it sanctions may not make knowledge unreachable or contaminate the knowledge produced. But they surely slow down the production of knowledge if the channeling is in the wrong direction. If the stereotype connecting blacks and violence were true, for example, the fastest way to discover that truth would doubtless be to investigate the stereotype directly. Not knowing whether the stereotype is true, however, the most plausible way to proceed would be to pursue multiple research programs—the stereotype-focused research program as well as West's egalitarian-value-directed research program, for example. Not only would this be the most efficient way to proceed, but it would also provide valuable comparative assessments of programs in addition to the direct empirical assessments available to each individual program. It would also provide the most thorough assessments, since one program might generate data relevant to another that the other had no access to itself, data with which it nevertheless has to deal. Pursuing multiple research programs would also make more likely the discovery of multiple causal factors and a more complex understanding of the subject at hand. Limiting science to 'socially responsible' research, by contrast, places unnecessary obstacles in the way of science's search for truth."

"That's not true!" gasps the candidate. "Socially responsible research, of course, cannot be guaranteed to produce truth. But neither can socially irresponsible research. Nor can socially responsible research—or socially irresponsible research—be guaranteed to be efficient in its search for truth, or more efficient than the other. We simply cannot say, a priori, what kind of research will produce the best results. If the stereotype connecting blacks and violence were true, for example, would scientists more likely discover that truth, or discover it more quickly or easily, if they explored all plausible ways in which blacks could be inherently disposed to violence, or would they more likely, or more quickly or easily, discover that truth if they explored all plausible social factors that could explain the dissimilarities in violence within the black and white communities? If it be said that the former 'direct' approach would obviously be better, it must be noted that many in the black community would not cooperate with that approach, whereas they would cooperate with the latter, socially responsible approach (see West 2002 and 2004 for the 'culture of silence' that has surrounded the problem of domestic violence in the black community, the reasons for it, and the methods that have proven valuable to overcome it). That lack of cooperation would have a profound effect on 'efficiency.' It must also be noted that the latter, socially responsible approach, no less than the other, could make use of multiple research programs, with all of the benefits those bestow. So the comparison would not have to be between (as you seemed to suggest) West's program plus the stereotype-focused research program on the one side versus West's program alone on the other. The socially responsible (second) side of the comparison could include, in addition to West's program, any number of other socially responsible alternative or complementary research programs. And of course, it would matter what all of these various research programs were like, which scientists were pursuing them, how much funding they had at their disposal, what background knowledge and conceptual and technological resources they could draw on, etc., etc. The upshot is that you simply cannot assume that limiting science to socially responsible research will slow science down in its search for truth."

"But what if it did?" the candidate continues. "What if the efficiency of research *were* compromised by the restrictions imposed by the ideal of socially responsible science? What grounds are there for saying that these restrictions would then constitute '*unnecessary* obstacles in the way of science's search for truth' when these restrictions—the social values like West's egalitarian values imposed by the ideal of socially responsible science—would be *justified*? Everyone concedes that the value of efficiency in research has its limits, that there are other values, including other social values, that are more important. It might be far more efficient for searching out the truth, for example, if scientists simply ignored the risks to human subjects or society or the environment posed by various lines of research and ethics committees and publishers and funders and the public at large allowed them to do so. But acting in this way would be unconscionable despite the epistemic efficiency it might offer. The ideal of socially responsible science simply extends these constraints already recognized as appropriate for science. In so doing, it does not sacrifice science as a genuine source of knowledge but merely acknowledges that science has other goals and other responsibilities besides its epistemic ones. Thus, it might be more efficient for searching out the truth about domestic violence in the black community if scientists pursued any research they pleased—for example, the stereotype-focused research program in addition to West's approach—irrespective of its effects on the black community. But acting in this way would again be unconscionable. After all, the stereotype-focused research program begins with a characterization of blacks born of prejudice, with no serious empirical backing, and dignifies it by making it the subject of scientific research. It thereby suggests that the characterization has some plausibility (if it had none, why would scientists bother to investigate it?). And so, the stereotype-focused research program helps to keep the stereotype alive, paradoxically, even while it may be accumulating evidence against that stereotype and as one result (there are others) decreases the likelihood that black women will receive the help they deserve to combat domestic violence. West's program, in contrast, does none of this—is explicitly designed to do just the opposite—even though it also, indirectly, investigates the stereotype. The difference is that West's program aims to help the black community with the knowledge it gathers and is in an excellent position to do just that. The stereotype-focused research program seems aimed to do just the opposite and is in an excellent position to do just that. Small wonder that West has received an award from the black community for the work she is doing—the Outstanding Researcher Award from the Institute on Domestic Violence in the African American Community—whereas it is safe to say that the stereotype-focused research program would meet with a very different response."

WHERE YOU COME TO A DECISION

Is it now clear that the ideal of socially responsible science can fulfill the epistemic role as well as the political role of the old ideal of value-free science?

"If it is," you reply, "that will still not suffice to justify embracing it. The reason the ideal of value-free science generally fell into disrepute, remember, was that it could not be put to use. Even what we take to be the greatest science failed to exemplify it, and sociologists and philosophers of science assured us that most science never would exemplify it, never could exemplify it. Something similar happened for feminist scientists as well, for they found that their science, though it clearly seemed more adequate than sexist science, still fell as far short of the ideal of value-free science as that sexist science. In short, the ideal of value-free science failed to be a viable ideal, useful for actual science. Is the ideal of socially responsible science similarly inapplicable?"

"Not at all," boasts the candidate. "Unlike value-free science, socially responsible science *is* possible. Indeed, it exists. As noted at the outset, feminist scientists such as West are among the scientists who are doing it. This does not mean that all that we currently consider the greatest science *is* socially responsible science. That has to be determined on a case-by-case basis, and feminist scientists and historians and philosophers of science, among others, have already done some of this work. But it does mean that there actually are concrete models available to other scientists and science policy makers that help to show them what the ideal of socially responsible science amounts to and how it can be put into practice. And it also means that—"

Here the candidate is interrupted by you, waxing impatient: "Questions concerning values—including the 'values that meet the needs of society,' the values that the ideal of socially responsible science aims to entrench in science—are highly controversial. Even feminists, who agree on so many things, are far from agreement concerning what their egalitarian social values amount to and how they can best be put into practice— for example, exactly what a gender-equal society would be like and how it should be pursued. So isn't the ideal of socially responsible science just as inapplicable as the ideal of value-free science, since no one can agree concerning what would satisfy it, concerning which values would meet the needs of society?"

"You are not *listening*," replies the candidate. "Of course, there is dis-agreement concerning values, including the 'values that meet the needs of society.' But there is also crucially important agreement, especially con-cerning the concrete issues that affect people's day-to-day lives. Regard-ing West's research, for example, it is uncontroversial that women deserve to live without fear of violence from domestic partners, the value that underlies West's research. But it is equally uncontroversial that women deserve to live without fear of rape, sexual harassment, incest, and other forms of violence directed at women and that women deserve equal edu-cational opportunities with men, equal employment opportunities with men, equal opportunities for health care, and so on. These values are not only uncontroversial in Western cultures, they are also attested to in the policy declarations and activities of such international organizations as the United Nations, the International Labour Organization, the World Health Organization, and Amnesty International. These are the kinds of shared values that motivate and inform feminist research in such fields as psychology, sociology, economics, political science, archaeology, anthro-pology, biology, and medical research. And this is the kind of research that exemplifies the ideal of socially responsible science."

"So your question should be," the candidate continues, "not *is* the ideal of socially responsible science applicable to real science under real (e.g., our current) social conditions but *how extensively* is this ideal applicable to this science under these conditions. That is to say, can the shared social values that shape the research of feminist scientists come to shape the research of other scientists as well, and can other social values that meet the needs of society but do not now shape research be added to them? These are large-scale empirical questions, but fortunately, there is enough empirical evi-dence currently available to at least begin to answer them. Certainly, the long-term flourishing of feminism in some fields (e.g., primatology, cultural anthropology, paleontology, and developmental biology) and its recent growth in others (e.g., archaeology) give cause for optimism. Primatology is a particularly good example (see, for what follows, Fedigan 2001). This field has wholeheartedly embraced feminist ways of doing research—in pursuing research that rescues female primates from their previous second-class status in the theoretical understandings of the field (as merely mothers, as merely passive resources for males), in pursuing research that answers questions of importance to women (e.g., regarding male parenting roles or the evolution of female sexuality), in pursuing research that uses new female-friendly conceptual tools (e.g., sampling methods that more readily include females), and so on. Primatology has embraced such feminist ways of doing research even though very few of its practitioners see themselves as feminists and even though the standard attitude of these practitioners is that politics does not belong in science. More significant, the reasons these practitioners give for doing so—that it makes for better *science*, that it is *scientifically* right to consider questions from a female as well as a male perspective, to research issues of concern to women as well as men, and about females as well as males—give cause to be hopeful that further applications of the ideal of socially responsible science are possible."

"But other fields tell a different story!" you interject.

The candidate falls silent for a moment, then continues: "Other fields have made some of the same changes as primatology but only under duress. U.S. medical research is an example. Only since 1993, when Congress passed the National Institutes of Health Revitalization Act, which mandated the inclusion of women and minority men in publicly funded U.S. biomedical research and made funding contingent on that inclusion, has the neglect of females in both basic and clinical research been curtailed. Earlier initiatives, such as NIH's 1986 guidelines requiring grant applications to include female subjects in medical testing and research, were generally ignored (Rosser 1994; Schiebinger 1999). And still other fields have made few, if any, changes—economics, for example, in which women's needs and priorities in the family as well as the larger society remain invisible or inadequately treated (Nelson 1996a and 1996b; Waring 1997; Ferber and Nelson 2003; Fineman and Dougherty 2005). Do these cases show that the ideal of socially responsible science is of limited applicability? Not at all. The case of U.S. medical research shows that economic incentives—not only public funding but very possibly also tax incentives for industry-funded science and conditions on the tax-exempt status of foundation-funded science—can be a powerful method to bring about socially responsible science. The case of economics shows that the need in some areas has never been greater. And both cases show that much hard work will have to be done to determine for each of the various fields of science how best to achieve what the ideal of socially responsible science recommends. But this is the kind of work that makes sense only if, and after, the ideal of socially responsible science is adopted. For this work will answer the question, not *how extensively* is the ideal of socially responsible science applicable, but *how* can it be made *more applicable*."

Do you have any more questions? Or is the examination over? And if so, what is its outcome? Has the ideal of socially responsible science shown both that it can fulfill the epistemic and political roles of the old ideal of value-free science and that it will actually get the job done, not fail to apply itself? Has it shown, in short, that it merits the position now vacated by the ideal of value-free science? Since I have put forward this candidate (and also argued in its defense), you should already know where I stand. But you have followed the examination as closely as I, and you have posed most of the questions, so you play a role here, too. Indeed, the decision, I think, now depends on you.

4

Challenges from Every Direction

Even if the ideal of socially responsible science passed the examination given to it in chapter 3, it still may not be worthy of acceptance. After all, the ideal of socially responsible science threatens serious societal interference with science—more serious societal interference, by far, than the other ideals considered—and this interference is simply not visible when we limit our attention to the case of feminist scientists injecting their own feminist values into their own research. The ideal of socially responsible science, remember, permits not all social values in science (like the social value management ideal of science) or no social values (like the ideal of value-free science) or only those social values, or associated standpoints, that produce scientific success (like the empiricist ideal of science); the ideal of socially responsible science permits only those social values in science that make for a good society, only those social values that can be morally justified. And there is a long tradition of reluctance—reluctance on the part of scientists and nonscientists alike—to sanction any such societal interference with science. This reluctance, in fact, is backed by five kinds of justification. The first—the epistemological justification—suggests that the more a practice is concerned with knowledge, especially technical knowledge such as science, the more it should be left in the hands of properly trained experts, free from societal control or oversight. The second—the historical justification—points to the dire social as well as epistemic effects that *have* resulted from societal interference with science—such as those that occurred in Stalinist Russia or Nazi Germany or Galileo's Italy. The third—the sociological justification—emphasizes the unique cognitive and social norms institutionalized in science that ultimately ensure the advancement of science, and the fourth—the economic justification—emphasizes the extraordinary socioeconomic progress that results from this advancement; according to these justifications, in short, societal interference in science is simply unnecessary. Finally, the fifth—the political justification—insists that scientists have a right to freedom of research just as they have a right to freedom of thought and freedom of speech and that societal interference with science infringes on that right. If the ideal of socially responsible science is to be worthy of acceptance, adequate responses to these five challenges must be provided.

THE EPISTEMOLOGICAL CHALLENGE

The idea that science should be free of societal interference is as old as modern science itself, and the epistemological justification of that idea has been the dominant one in its defense. Indeed, the epistemological justification has been associated with such illustrious individuals as Tommaso Campanella (who wrote *The Defense of Galileo* in 1616, published in 1622), René Descartes, John Milton, and Baruch de Spinoza in the early modern period, and John Stuart Mill, Michael Polanyi, Imre Lakatos, and Thomas Kuhn in more recent times, to name just a few (Wilholt forthcoming). All of these individuals have elaborated optimal strategies for acquiring knowledge, and all of the optimal strategies preclude societal interference. The problem is that the various optimal strategies also tend to conflict. In fact, just about the only thing these strategies agree on is that societal interference in knowledge production should be avoided. Consider a few—the most influential—examples.

First, John Stuart Mill's famous "marketplace of ideas"[1] strategy, the strategy according to which the acquisition of knowledge requires the free investigation of all ideas:

> The peculiar evil of silencing the expression of an opinion is that it is robbing the human race, posterity as well as the existing generation—those who dissent from the opinion, still more than those who hold it. If the opinion is right, they are deprived of the opportunity of exchanging error for truth; if wrong, they lose, what is almost as great a benefit, the clearer perception and livelier impression of truth produced by its collision with error. (Mill [1859] 1956, 21)

Unpopular ideas need especially to be investigated:

> [Society] practices a social tyranny more formidable than many kinds of political oppression, since, though not usually upheld by such extreme penalties, it leaves fewer means of escape, penetrating much more deeply into the details of life, and enslaving the soul itself. Protection, therefore, against the tyranny of the magistrate is not enough; there needs protection also against the tyranny of the prevailing opinion and feeling, against the tendency of society to impose, by other means than civil penalties, its own ideas and practices as rules of conduct on those who dissent from them. (7)

And ideas, popular and unpopular alike, need to continue being investigated, even after they have been found wanting. For individuals are not infallible, and "ages are no more infallible than individuals—every age having held many opinions which subsequent ages have deemed not only false but absurd; and it is as certain that many opinions, now general, will be rejected by future ages, as it is that many, once general, are rejected by the present" (23). The upshot is that the ideal of socially responsible science, in gearing research in certain (egalitarian, environment-friendly,

---

1. Jill Gordon (1997) shows that this description is a misnomer, however.

peace-friendly, etc.) directions and not others, is fraught with epistemic danger. It is also unnecessary, at least in the long run:

> The real advantage which truth has consists in this, that when an opinion is true, it may be extinguished once, twice, or many times, but in the course of ages there will generally be found persons to rediscover it, until some one of its reappearances falls on a time when from favourable circumstances it escapes persecution until it has made such head as to withstand all subsequent attempts to suppress it. (36)

For Mill, then, the optimal strategy for pursuing knowledge is to allow what has been called a free marketplace of ideas. For Thomas Kuhn, on the other hand, the optimal strategy is just the opposite:

> As a glance at any Baconian natural history or a survey of the pre-paradigm development of any science will show, nature is vastly too complex to be explored even approximately at random. Something must tell the scientist where to look and what to look for, and that something, though it may not last beyond his generation, is the paradigm with which his education as a scientist has supplied him. (Kuhn 1963, 363)

Indeed, for Kuhn, effective knowledge seeking scarcely begins before a community of inquirers can take for granted a particular way of viewing the world and of practicing science within it and turn its attention to more esoteric questions of detail. Only then is the community engaging in "normal" science, "mature" science, what Kuhn calls "paradigm-directed" science. And this holds even though there is an element of the arbitrary (what Mill would call fallibility) in the particular paradigm the community has adopted as the foundation of its practice:

> When examining normal science . . . , we shall want finally to describe that research as a strenuous and devoted attempt to force nature into the conceptual boxes supplied by professional education. Simultaneously, we shall wonder whether research could proceed without such boxes, whatever the element of arbitrariness in their historic origins and, occasionally, in their subsequent development. (Kuhn 1962, 5)

Nevertheless, although Kuhn defends this monistic, largely "dogmatic" approach to knowledge seeking in contradistinction to Mill's pluralistic, "free market" approach, he comes to the same conclusion as Mill regarding the inadvisability of societal interference with science:

> One of the things a scientific community acquires with a paradigm is a criterion for choosing problems ["puzzles"] that, while the paradigm is taken for granted, can be assumed to have solutions. To a great extent these are the only problems that the community will admit as scientific or encourage its members to undertake. . . . A paradigm can, for that matter, even insulate the community from those socially important problems that are not reducible to the puzzle form, because they cannot be stated in terms of the conceptual and instrumental tools the paradigm supplies. Such problems can be a distraction. . . . One of the reasons why normal science seems to progress so rapidly is that its

practitioners concentrate on problems that only their own lack of ingenuity should keep them from solving. (1962, 37)

Michael Polanyi puts the conclusion more starkly:

I appreciate the generous sentiments which actuate the aspiration of guiding the progress of science into socially beneficent channels, but I hold its aim to be impossible and nonsensical. . . . Any attempt at guiding scientific research towards a purpose other than its own is an attempt to deflect it from the advancement of science. . . . You can kill or mutilate the advance of science, you cannot shape it. (Polanyi 1962, 62)

Polanyi's rationale, however, is the unpredictability of science: science "can advance only by essentially unpredictable steps, pursuing problems of its own, and the practical benefits of these advances will be incidental and hence doubly unpredictable" (1962, 62). More particularly, Polanyi suggests that science is a cooperative enterprise of independent explorers who coordinate their activities by responding to one another's achievements—much like a group of individuals who put together the pieces of a jigsaw puzzle in full view of one another, "so that every time a piece of it is fitted in by one helper, all the others will immediately watch out for the next step that becomes possible in consequence."

Such self-coordination of independent initiatives leads to a joint result which is unpremeditated by any of those who bring it about. Their coordination is guided as by "an invisible hand" towards the joint discovery of a hidden system of things. Since its end-result is unknown, this kind of cooperation can only advance stepwise, and the total performance will be the best possible if each consecutive step is decided upon by the person most competent to do so. (1962, 55)

The pursuit of science can be organized, therefore, in no other manner than by granting complete independence to all mature scientists. They will then distribute themselves over the whole field of possible discoveries, each applying his own special ability to the task that appears most profitable to him. (1951, 89)

And, therefore, the "present practice of filling vacant chairs by the most eminent candidate that the university can attract," irrespective of the candidate's specialization or the social needs such specialization might serve, is "the best safeguard for rational distribution of efforts over rival lines of scientific research" (1962, 64).

For Polanyi, then, the unpredictability of science is key to its need for autonomy. Only free of the interference of society can science hope to uncover the "hidden system of things." How different from Kuhn! For Kuhn, science is normally highly predictable—an articulation of the known (a scientific community's accepted paradigm) rather than an exploration of the unknown:[2]

---

2. Interestingly enough, Kuhn also uses the analogy of puzzle solving to explain what scientists do, but for him, constructing the joint jigsaw puzzle is more like a game of skill in which the overall (paradigm-provided) picture is quite unimportant, each scientist already knowing what that final picture looks like.

Perhaps the most striking feature of . . . normal research problems . . . is how little they aim to produce major novelties, conceptual or phenomenal. Sometimes, as in a wave-length measurement, everything but the most esoteric detail of the result is known in advance, and the typical latitude of expectation is only somewhat wider. (Kuhn 1962, 35)

And for Kuhn, uncovering a hidden reality is not what science is about:

The developmental process described in this essay [*The Structure of Scientific Revolutions*] has been a process of evolution *from* primitive beginnings—a process whose successive stages [of paradigm-directed normal science punctuated by noncumulative revolutionary breaks] are characterized by an increasingly detailed and refined understanding of nature. But nothing that has been or will be said makes it a process of evolution *toward* anything. . . . We are all deeply accustomed to seeing science as the one enterprise that draws constantly nearer to some goal set by nature in advance.
    But need there be any such goal? (1962, 170–171)

Nonetheless, for both Polanyi and Kuhn, science manifests an internal dynamic that must not be tampered with lest scientific progress be slowed down or even halted altogether.

Polanyi's rationale for shielding science from societal interference is thus as different from Kuhn's as Kuhn's is different from Mill's. Indeed, all three rationales in fundamental ways conflict with one another, and while each rationale is made to seem convincing by its author, their mutual conflicts at the same time call each into question. Nevertheless, these rationales are frequently used to justify the policy of societal non-interference with science. Witness just one example, that of political scientist Don K. Price, founding dean of Harvard University's Kennedy School of Government and for many years advisor to the U.S. Executive Branch on governmental organization and administration, who cites in defense of societal noninterference with science *both* Polanyi and Kuhn:

Basic science is quite unlike politics in the way in which it refuses to be responsible for following a purpose. . . .
    It is reasonably obvious that each scientific department in the universities of the highest rank neither apportions its budget, nor makes its principal permanent-tenure appointments, mainly by calculating the social and economic benefits to be gained from the decision. It makes such decisions by judging how much the work of a particular scientist, or a particular group of scientists, is going to advance knowledge or understanding.
    The incidental effect of this approach is to put the issue on a basis that strengthens the case for the independence and self-government of science. . . . As long . . . as the most respected faculty positions are awarded on the basis of the candidates' contributions to the discipline, the permanent-tenure appointments—the key actions that determine the whole structure of influence within the field—are bound to be made by the scientists themselves. And they are made on the basis of considerations that are hardly related at all to the interests

of the layman or the general citizen. [Price cites Polanyi's "The Republic of
Science" here.]

But the essential purpose of this approach is not hostility to those interests.
On the contrary the approach is related to the intellectual structure of science
and its system of motivation. Science, in setting its goals and measuring its
progress in ways that do not correspond to the layman's purposes, does not do
so in order to escape political responsibility; it seeks to escape such responsibility in order to be free to discover the most fruitful ways to advance knowledge.
The body of accepted theory within a discipline, and the system of assumptions and tools with which it works, set the standards to which the scientist
must conform in order to advance in reputation and influence. Modern science
makes rapid progress because in this way each discipline chooses the problems
which it encourages its members to undertake. . . . This is a way of protecting
the scientist from being asked to do things that are socially important—important in the sense that a layman would like to see them done, even if a miracle
were needed to accomplish them—but that do not seem currently within the
potential scope of scientific techniques. [Price cites Kuhn's *Structure of Scientific Revolutions* here.] (D. K. Price 1965, 175–177)[3]

But why should "the advance of knowledge" be defined solely in terms
of the interests of (socially unconcerned) scientists and not at all in terms
of the needs of society, especially when (as Kuhn would have it) that
advance may have little, if anything, to do with the uncovering of an
independent reality? And if the advance of knowledge *is* defined, at least
in part, in terms of the needs of society, then why must the kind of societal interference called for by the ideal of socially responsible science
necessarily be a hindrance to that advance? Indeed, even if the advance
of knowledge is defined solely in terms of the interests of (socially unconcerned) scientists, why must the societal interference called for by the
ideal of socially responsible science necessarily be a hindrance? Whether
it is or not would have to be determined on the basis of empirical evidence, not on the basis of the kind of conflicting a priori argumentation
offered by Mill, Kuhn, and Polanyi—empirical evidence showing that
societal interference does cause a cessation or at least a slowdown of scientific progress. Unfortunately, neither these thinkers nor their followers,
such as Price, provide such empirical evidence. For that, we must turn to
an analysis of history.

THE HISTORICAL CHALLENGE

Unlike the epistemological challenge to societal interference with science, the historical challenge focuses on particular episodes of scientific

knowledge production rather than on general strategies for producing knowledge. And unlike the general strategies of the epistemological challenge, the burden of these particular episodes is noncontroversial. Everyone agrees, after all, that Lysenko's science represented the sapping of scientific progress in biology in the Soviet Union from the 1930s to the 1960s and that it was associated with state interference with science, everyone agrees that Nazi interference with science perverted German science during the Third Reich, everyone agrees that the Roman Catholic Church's interference with science in Galileo's time formed a serious obstacle to scientific progress, and so on. These well-known historical cases, though few, are so alarming that they have motivated a profound skepticism regarding any mode of societal interference with science. But what do these cases actually justify regarding that particular mode of interference represented by the ideal of socially responsible science?

Consider, first, the case of Lysenko (see, for what follows, Lewontin and Levins 1976; Graham 1987; and Roll-Hansen 2005). According to the ideal of socially responsible science, science should be judged by two kinds of standards, by moral/political standards as well as by epistemic standards. That is, science should be found wanting if it fails sound epistemic requirements, but it should also be found wanting if it is shaped by unacceptable social values; and only when both kinds of requirements are fulfilled should talk of scientific advance or scientific progress be considered appropriate. In the case of Lysenko's science, however, both kinds of requirements were not fulfilled.

Start with the social requirements. By the end of the 1920s—it was then that the short-lived Russian eugenics movement had come to a close under heavy pressure from the political authorities—the attempt to explain human behavior in terms of innate characteristics was considered illegitimate in the Soviet Union. Instead, social environment was billed as the most important influence on human behavior, and all major writers on psychology and education until the late 1960s emphasized their ability to mold the personalities and talents of children by constructing a suitable social environment. Crime, alcoholism, prostitution, and other social ills were expected to vanish under the influence of the right educational and political and economic conditions. This was, at any rate, the social/scientific goal—human perfectibility, social equality, the "new Soviet man"—and it contrasted sharply with what was widely understood to be the elitist message of classical genetics: that genes determine traits and abilities, that genes are (relatively) immutable, and hence that the social hierarchy traits and abilities determine is also (relatively) immutable. (Note that it had been distinguished geneticists such as Hermann Muller, Nikolai Koltsov, Nikolai Vavilov, and Aleksandr Serebrovskii who favored Soviet eugenics programs—e.g., Serebrovskii proposed large-scale artificial insemination of Soviet women with the sperm of outstanding men.)

Trofim Lysenko's agricultural research, concerned with the directed transformation of biological varieties (interpreted as the directed transformation
of heredity) by means of environmental manipulation, fit right in with the
new social/scientific goal, although neither he nor his followers typically
applied his results to the human case.[4] Lysenko's research also fit in with
the goal's methodological underpinnings: the Marxist unity of theory and
practice, the view that scientific research should have a clear social purpose by being tied to the needs of society and should be evaluated thereby
(the "practice" criterion of scientific truth). Geneticists such as Muller,
Koltsov, Vavilov, and Serebrovskii had been members of the intellectual
middle classes of prerevolutionary Russia and the rift these individuals
took for granted between their frequently highly theoretical research and
agricultural practice was, as one observer of the time described it, "a capi-
talist remnant in the mind of the individual scientific workers," which
made them "lock themselves up in their laboratories and not move further
than their greenhouses" (Aleksandr Muralov, quoted in Roll-Hansen 2005,
101). By contrast, Lysenko, who came from peasant origins and received
the bulk of his technical training after the revolution, aimed to and did use
the state and collective farms as his laboratory, directly involving the peasants and their farming experience with his research and not only with its
results. For him, large-scale practical experience was superior to "pure"
scientific experiments in deciding the truth of theories. "In every aspect
the conflict in agriculture was a revolutionary conflict, posing the detached,
elite, theoretical, pure scientific, educated values of the old middle classes
against the engaged, enthusiastic, practical, applied, self-taught values of
the new holders of power" (Lewontin and Levins 1976, 51).

The social values of Lysenko's research program, then, had much to
recommend them. Not so the epistemic values. To begin with, the concepts Lysenko relied on were extremely vague. *Vernalization*, for example,
one of Lysenko's key concepts, covered almost anything that was done to
seeds or tubers before planting; *nutrient* seemed to include everything
from chemical elements in the soil or organic food or gases present in the
atmosphere to environmental conditions such as sunlight, temperature,
and humidity; and his theory of phasic development of plants never
clearly differentiated or coherently described the different plant phases
he was proposing. Lysenko's experimental failings were more worrisome
than his conceptual failings, however. His claim to have converted the
winter wheat *Kooperatorka* into a spring wheat, for example, was based on

---

4. The human case cropped up, however. Thus, for example, when Muller called attention to "the fascist race and class implications of Lamarckism, since if true it would imply the
genetic inferiority, at present, of peoples and classes that had lived under conditions giving
less opportunity for mental and physical development," Yakovlev replied that "the genes of
man had been changed by the environment of civilization and therefore primitive races
existing today have inferior genes. But . . . about three generations of socialism will so change
the genes as to make all races equal. Just better the conditions and you better the genes."
(Hermann Muller, in a letter to Julian Huxley, as quoted in Roll-Hansen 2005, 203, 214).

a year-and-a-half-long experiment with a single plant and its offspring (the experiment started with two plants, but one perished because of "pests gnawing its roots"; quoted in Roll-Hansen 2005, 201), an experiment whose results were never duplicated either inside or outside the Soviet Union. Experiments involving larger samples had other problems: "in the conditions of Soviet farms, where there was often no electricity and no refrigerating equipment, it must have been nearly impossible to keep the seeds in uniform conditions over long periods of time" (Graham 1987, 109), and experimental conditions frequently presented an ideal environment for the spread of fungi and plant diseases. What's more, the Russian plant varieties used in these experiments were of unknown (and doubtful) purity, and there was an almost total absence of control plots (Lysenko frequently presented his evidence in terms of yields in a certain season with both treated and untreated plantings of the same crops, but the comparisons were not rigorous enough to serve as controlled samples). Finally, extremely inaccurate records were kept of trials, and diverse ways to discount negative results were readily available (peasants' lack of cooperation with extremely labor-intensive procedures, impure plant varieties, plant diseases, variable weather conditions, and more). Risky predictions were not made in any case. For example,

> Vernalization was only very rarely used as an attempt to make possible the previously impossible—growing crops that had never been grown before in the region because of the climate. Rather, it was usually directed toward making traditional crops ripen earlier or growing a grain that because of the length of its growing season could only occasionally be successfully harvested by traditional methods in a certain region before frost. These are the kinds of experiments in which the evidence can be manipulated very easily, or where sloppiness in record-keeping can conceal results from even an honest researcher. (Graham 1987, 110)[5]

The upshot is that the epistemic requirements of the ideal of socially responsible science were not fulfilled by Lysenko's science even if the social requirements were, and hence, the failure of Lysenko's science forms no critique of the ideal of socially responsible science. Lysenko's science is simply not the kind of enterprise recommended by the ideal of socially responsible science. This holds especially of the Stalinist tactics used to

5. Even Nils Roll-Hansen, who takes Loren Graham as well as other historians to task for at times insufficiently recognizing "the strength of valid scientific support for parts of Lysenko's work" (2005, 293) and aims, instead, to give a more balanced perspective on Lysenko, clearly acknowledges in the end Lysenko's "unscientific methods of experimenting and arguing" (295). Richard Lewontin and Richard Levins also provide an especially open-minded and sympathetic portrayal of Lysenko, though they still conclude that "in the end, the Lysenkoist revolution was a failure. It did not result in a radical breakthrough in agricultural productivity. Far from overthrowing traditional genetics and creating a new science, it cut short the pioneering work of Soviet genetics and set it back a generation. Its own contribution to contemporary biology was negligible" (1976, 33).

ensure the survival of Lysenkoism and the suppression of its competitors: the elaborate system of formal censorship, the informal self-censorship created by constant threats of terror and political reprisals, the loss of professional positions, the imprisonments, the executions. Such tactics are not mandated by the ideal of socially responsible science any more than they are mandated by any of the other ideals of science discussed in chapter 3. Indeed, scientists can be imprisoned for supporting any social values in research or for supporting empirically unsuccessful values in research, just as they can be imprisoned for supporting socially irresponsible values in research. And they can be imprisoned for not supporting a diversity of values in research. But neither the ideal of value-free science nor the ideal of socially responsible science nor Longino's social value management ideal of science nor the empiricist ideal of science mandates such a mode of enforcement of its prescriptions. And certainly, the ideal of socially responsible science mandates no mode of enforcement that violates its epistemic prescriptions while it supports its social prescriptions, as was the case with Lysenko's science.

The case of Lysenko, then, does not present a genuine challenge to the ideal of socially responsible science. Neither does the case of the Nazis (see, for what follows, Deichmann 1996; Proctor 1988, 1999, and 2000; Jewish Virtual Library 2007). True, it was said in Germany under Hitler, as it was in the Soviet Union under Stalin, that the goal of science was to serve the people; and true, the science that was done in Germany did tend to be much more impressive from an epistemic point of view than Lysenko's science—tended, in fact, to succeed in fulfilling the epistemic requirements of the ideal of socially responsible science. But in Germany, "serving the people" was understood in a very peculiar way. Indeed, in Germany, it was biology, not social environment, that was held to be the most important determinant of human character and human institutions, and hence, if problems were found in the latter (human character or institutions), the causes and cures would have to be found in the former (human biology). In particular, the economic and social problems facing Germany after World War I were traced to such factors as the "degeneration" of the "German racial stock" or the ill health of the "German genetic streams," and the solution to these problems was said to lie in "racial hygiene" or "racial cleansing," isolating and removing the causes of the degeneration. Hence, the miscegenation laws banning marriage between Germans (Aryans) and Jews and between "healthy" Germans and Germans with afflictions such as venereal disease or feeble-mindedness; the sterilization of alcoholics and those with hereditary diseases such as schizophrenia; the euthanasia of retarded and handicapped children and adult psychiatric patients; the expulsion of Jews from professional life and their segregation in ghettos; and, finally, the extermination of Jews and gypsies and homosexuals, Communists, the handicapped, prostitutes, drug addicts, the homeless, the tubercular, and anyone else stigmatized by German racial scientists as "degenerate" (*Lebensunwertes Leben* or "life unworthy of life")—the "final solution."

In Germany under Hitler, in short, serving the people meant serving—perfecting—the "race," that is, serving some of the people while ignoring the good of, devaluing, enslaving, and finally murdering the rest of the people. And to the extent that the science that was done in Germany at this time was shaped by the goal of serving the people understood in this way, it most definitely did not fulfill the social requirements of the ideal of socially responsible science, even if it did fulfill the epistemic requirements. But how extensive was the failure? It obviously included all the science done in Nazi concentration camps—the experiments to investigate the effectiveness of various kinds of vaccines and other chemical substances on inmates who were deliberately infected with malaria, typhus, yellow fever, smallpox, cholera, diphtheria, or other diseases; the experiments to investigate the effectiveness of various treatments for hypothermia on inmates exposed for hours to freezing temperatures (which included investigating how long it took to lower the body temperature to death and at what temperature death occurred); the experiments to investigate the effectiveness of various treatments for wounds and burns previously inflicted on inmates and deliberately infected with bacteria such as streptococcus, gas gangrene, and tetanus (sometimes aggravated by forcing wood shavings and ground glass into the wounds); the experiments to investigate the effects of various poisons; to determine the easiest and quickest methods to sterilize millions of people; and so forth. All this science obviously failed to fulfill the social requirements of the ideal of socially responsible science. But all kinds of other German science failed as well, all the racially related genetic and biomedical and anthropological and psychological research (e.g., into the links between Jews and criminal behavior, Jews and mental infirmity, Jews and homosexuality, and Jews and the dangers of racial miscegenation) and all the military-related physical and chemical and biological research (e.g., into atomic fission and advanced ballistic missiles and nerve gas). Even apparently progressive public-health-related research failed to fulfill the social requirements of the ideal of socially responsible science. For example, German cancer research, at the time the most advanced in the world, motivated the introduction of such health reforms as smoke-free public spaces, bans on carcinogenic food dyes, and new means of controlling occupational carcinogens. But this research was promoted and shaped by Nazi ideals of bodily purity and racial hygiene, and it was suffused with Nazi rhetoric (as when the nascent tumor was characterized as "a new race of cells, distinct from the other cell races of the body," a pathological race that needed to be destroyed; Proctor 1999, 47). "The Nazi campaign against carcinogenic food dyes, the world-class asbestos and tobacco epidemiology, and much else as well, are all in some sense as fascist as the yellow stars and the death camps" (Proctor 2000, 345). And as for the rest of German science during the Third Reich, it was characterized by widespread accommodation and cooperation with the Nazi authorities:

> When Hitler was preparing his seizure of power, he figured the German scientists into the equation as a *quantité négligeable*, and unfortunately he was right. I cannot shake the tormenting thought that it would have been possible to prevent much if, at the first moment Hitler attacked freedom and justice, a group of German scientists had protested (geneticist and wartime director of the Kaiser Wilhelm Institute for Biology Alfred Kuhn, quoted in Deichmann 1996, 318)

The flourishing of Nazi science was, then, no more an instance of the ideal of socially responsible science—and hence no more a challenge to that ideal—than the flourishing of Lysenko's science. Nor was the lack of flourishing of Galileo's science. Indeed, the case of Galileo involved, not social values applauded by the ideal of socially responsible science being imposed on science to damaging effect, but unacceptable epistemic values being imposed instead—in particular, the epistemic value of appealing to the "author" of the revealed words in the scriptures as the guarantor of their truth. "Galileo's Copernican challenge to the traditional worldview involved, at a quite fundamental level, a new set of scientific methods of determining truth." This challenge to the absolute priority of the traditional method of determining truth through revelation posed a threat to religion

> as foundational as one could get, since the entire set of religious beliefs, as well as the complex of institutions based upon them, are grounded in the acceptance of this authority. . . . Seen in this context the primary focus of the Galileo trial was thus the issue of authority. . . . And the Galileo case has continued to this day to be of perennial interest because, even after the issue of Copernicanism has long been settled, the problem of the interaction between the authority of scientific reason and the authority of religious revelation has lived on, as science and religion have remained major cultural forces. The credibility of religious authority is what the trial was, and still is, about. (Blackwell 2006, 102)

Of course, the case of Galileo is a very complex affair, and historians of science have provided diverse interpretations of it involving other conflicts besides the conflict between science and scripture: conflicts between underlying realist and instrumentalist philosophies of science (Duhem [1908] 1969), conflicts over matters of patronage (Westfall 1989; Biagioli 1993), and conflicts within the post-Tridentine Church (Feldhay 1995), to cite only three examples. But "on almost any interpretation of this affair, the fundamental issue between Galileo and the Roman Catholic Church was conflict about questions of intellectual authority" (Osler 1998, 95), and that is of little bearing to the ideal of socially responsible science.

What conclusion can we then draw from these historic cases? Surely not that societal interference with science should be avoided. After all, compared with the Soviet Union, there was relatively little societal interference with science in Germany under National Socialism[6]—indeed, scientists were largely running the show.

> Science (especially biomedical science) under the Nazis cannot simply be seen in terms of a fundamentally "passive" or "apolitical" scientific community responding to purely external political forces; on the contrary, there is strong evidence that scientists actively designed and administered central aspects of National Socialist racial policy. (Proctor 1988, 6)

Societal interference—good societal interference promoting good social values—in this case could have helped, and its absence surely hurt. In the case of Lysenko's and Galileo's sciences, on the other hand, societal interference did hurt, since it served to enforce poor epistemic values on science, though a kind of interference that promoted good epistemic values while also promoting good social values—a kind of interference shaped by the ideal of socially responsible science, for example—could have helped.

THE SOCIOLOGICAL AND ECONOMIC CHALLENGES

But what if there had been no societal interference with science in Nazi Germany and the Soviet Union—no promotion of good social and epistemic values but also no promotion of bad values, either? What if nothing had compromised the institutionalized values and norms of science from effectively functioning? According to the sociological challenge to societal interference with science, the science that resulted would have been free of the flaws that dogged Lysenko's science and Nazi science, and according to the economic challenge to societal interference, that science would also have produced great social benefits. According to the sociological and economic challenges, in short, the aims motivating the adoption of the ideal of socially responsible science would have been satisfied by simply leaving science alone. Is this, then, the final verdict regarding the ideal of socially responsible science, that it is, at best, completely unnecessary? What grounds are there for saying that it is?

Consider, first, the sociological challenge. Its classic formulation was given in 1942 by one of the main architects of modern sociology, Robert K. Merton. According to Merton, the institution of science is marked by a

---

6. True, scientists were removed from their positions in both the Soviet Union and Nazi Germany, but they tended to be removed because of the nature of their scientific work in the Soviet Union, whereas they were removed because of their "race," irrespective of their scientific work (which was, however, racially characterized, e.g., as "Jewish science"), in Nazi Germany. And true, many of the scientists in the Soviet Union were sympathetic to the political directions in which science was being taken by Stalin. But when these scientists became openly critical of the epistemic weaknesses of Lysenko's science, they were imprisoned or executed nonetheless, despite their political sympathies.

distinctive "ethos" or "affectively toned complex of values and norms which is held to be binding on the man of science" ([1942] 1973, 268–269). This ethos, composed of both cognitive and social elements, is transmitted "by precept and example" and reinforced by rewards and punishments. And it is legitimized by the goal of science which it serves, "the extension of certified knowledge" (269–270). Although this ethos has never been codified, still, Merton assured us, "it can be inferred from the moral consensus of scientists as expressed in use and wont, in countless writings on the scientific spirit and in moral indignation directed toward contraventions of the ethos" (269). Merton initially suggested that four sets of norms and values make up the ethos of science, but fifteen years later (Merton [1957] 1973), he added others (e.g., "originality" and "humility"). The original four—"communism," "universalism," "disinterestedness," and "organized skepticism" (collectively nicknamed CUDOS by others)—were for Merton, however, the core of the ethos of science.

"Communism" referred to the requirement, institutionalized in scientific practice, that scientific knowledge should be part of the public domain, with recognition and esteem the sole property right of scientists. "The substantive findings of science are a product of social collaboration and are assigned to the community. They constitute a common heritage" (Merton [1942] 1973, 273). They also reflect a common heritage. "Newton's remark—'If I have seen farther it is by standing on the shoulders of giants'—expresses at once a sense of indebtedness to the common heritage and a recognition of the essentially cooperative and selectively cumulative quality of scientific achievement" (274–275). As a result, the findings of scientists must be shared with the whole community, and, of course, this aids in the advancement of knowledge. "Secrecy is the antithesis of this norm; full and open communication its enactment" (274).

"Universalism" referred to the requirement that scientific contributions be evaluated in accordance with "preestablished impersonal criteria" such as consistency with adequate and reliable empirical evidence and consistency with previously confirmed knowledge. The social attributes ("particularities") of contributors—their race, class origins, religion, gender, personal qualities, and the like—are to be treated as irrelevant in such evaluations. "Objectivity precludes particularism. . . . The imperative of universalism is rooted deep in the impersonal character of science" (270). The norm of universalism also referred to the demand that free access be granted to all scientific pursuits and that scientists be rewarded according to their contributions. "To restrict scientific careers on grounds other than lack of competence is to prejudice the furtherance of knowledge" (272).

"Disinterestedness," like universalism and communism, was an institutional imperative, not an individual one. It referred not to the motives (e.g., a passion for knowledge rather than fame and riches) that need to direct individual scientists so as to advance scientific knowledge but to the institutional control over those motives, whatever they are. "Scientific research is under the exacting scrutiny of fellow experts. Otherwise put . . . the activities of scientists are subject to rigorous policing, to a degree perhaps unparalleled in any other field of activity. The demand for disinterested-ness has a firm basis in the public and testable character of science" (276).

"Organized skepticism" again referred to an institutional imperative, not an individual one (e.g., scientists' skeptical attitudes toward their own work), namely, the "suspension of judgment" until the requisite evidence is in, realized through such institutional arrangements as the refereeing of work by competent peers. Since organized skepticism mandates the "detached scrutiny of beliefs in terms of empirical and logical criteria," free from outside (e.g., religious or political) influence, it "does not preserve the cleavage between the sacred and the profane, between that which requires uncritical respect and that which can be objectively analyzed" (277–278).

With norms such as communism, universalism, disinterestedness, and organized skepticism in place and undisturbed by societal interference, would the epistemic and moral failures of Lysenko's science and Nazi science have occurred? Communism should have precluded the secrecy of the experiments that were conducted in Nazi concentration camps and psychiatric institutions and, hopefully, the experiments themselves once the worldwide scientific community gained knowledge of them. Univer-salism should have precluded the removal of Jewish scientists from their positions in Nazi Germany and the devaluation of their work as "Jewish science," and it should also have precluded the devaluation of "bourgeois" scientists (such as Albert Einstein) and "bourgeois" science (such as quan-tum mechanics) in the Soviet Union. Disinterestedness should have pre-cluded Lysenko's power to denounce, deservedly or not, any and all scientists who disagreed with him and flourish as a scientist in the Soviet scientific community nonetheless. And organized skepticism should have precluded the widespread acceptance of Nazi racial theories within the scientific community in Germany, and it should have precluded the wholesale rejection of genetics in the Soviet Union even after the rest of the world was convinced of its worth. And so on. Merton emphasized, however, that "the institution of science is part of a larger social structure with which it is not always integrated. When the larger culture opposes universalism"—or communism or disinterestedness or organized skepticism— "the ethos of science is subjected to serious strain" (271). According to Merton, this is what happened with the totalitarian systems of Nazi Ger-many and the Soviet Union. When the institution of science is situated within a liberal democratic system, on the other hand, "a substantial sphere of autonomy—varying in extent, to be sure—is enjoyed by [science]" (Merton [1938] 1973, 258). And under such autonomy-favoring condi-tions, the advancement of science is more assured. So runs the sociological challenge to societal interference with science.

According to the economic challenge, moreover, when the advance-ment of science is assured, so is socioeconomic progress. Consider, for example, Vannevar Bush's *Science—The Endless Frontier: Report to the President on a Program for Postwar Scientific Research*, generally considered the most important, and certainly the most famous, contribution to the architecture of American science during the second half of the twentieth century. According to this report:

> Advances in science when put to practical use mean more jobs, higher wages, shorter hours, more abundant crops, more leisure for recreation, for study, for learning how to live without the deadening drudgery which has been the burden of the common man for ages past. Advances in science will also bring higher standards of living, will lead to the prevention or cure of diseases, will promote conservation of our limited national resources, and will assure means of defense against aggression. (Bush 1945, 5)

By contrast, "without scientific progress no amount of achievement in other directions can insure our health, prosperity, and security as a nation in the modern world" (6).

But exactly how will science produce all of these benefits? Central to the answer Bush gave was the notion of basic research. This was research "performed without thought of practical ends" that "results in general knowledge and an understanding of nature and its laws" (13). It was research, moreover, that was "unpredictable" (75): "One of the peculiarities of basic science is the variety of paths which lead to productive advance. Many of the most important discoveries have come as a result of experiments undertaken with quite different purposes in mind" (13). And finally, it was research that "requires special protection and specially assured [public] support" (77). "Pure research demands from its followers the freedom of mind to look at familiar facts from unfamiliar points of view. It does not always lend itself to organized efforts and is refractory to direction from above. In fact, nowhere else is the principle of freedom more important for significant achievement" (75–76). As a result, the public support of such research—"this is of the utmost importance"—"must leave the internal control of policy, personnel, and the method and scope of the research to the institutions themselves" in which the research is done (i.e., public and private colleges, universities, and research institutes) and ultimately to the individuals themselves who do the research (27). Nonetheless, public support must be continuous and substantial: "Basic research is a long-term process—it ceases to be basic if immediate results are expected on short-term support" (27).

It was scientific research of just this kind that the Bush report maintained would fuel not only applied science but also, ultimately, the technological innovations destined to meet society's economic, health, defense, and other needs:

> Basic research . . . provides scientific capital. It creates the fund from which the practical applications of knowledge must be drawn. New products and new processes do not appear full-grown. They are founded on new principles and new conceptions, which in turn are painstakingly developed by research in the purest realms of science.
>
> Today, it is truer than ever that basic research is the pacemaker of technological progress. (13–14; see also 68)

This idea that basic research fuels applied research, which fuels technological innovation and development, which fuels socioeconomic progress has come to be known as the linear model of innovation, and the related idea that society should provide continuous and substantial support for such basic research—without, however, interfering with it—in exchange for the socioeconomic benefits that flow from it has come to be known as the social contract for science.

According to the economic challenge to societal interference with science, then, the progress of science will yield an unlimited array of social benefits, and according to the sociological challenge, the ethos of science will facilitate that progress—assuming, that is, that science is left free of societal interference. According to the sociological and economic challenges, in short, the aims motivating the adoption of the ideal of socially responsible science will be satisfied without the adoption of that ideal, rendering it completely unnecessary. The problem, however, is that the sociological and economic challenges rest on sweeping empirical claims—that a Mertonian ethos of science is entrenched in scientific practice and facilitates scientific progress, that scientific progress leads to technological innovation and development, and that technological innovation and development leads to the kinds of social benefits demanded by the ideal of socially responsible science. Are these sweeping empirical claims justified?

Consider the first claim. Now granted, when we ask whether a Mertonian ethos of science is entrenched in scientific practice, we must keep in mind that this ethos "specifies shared expectations or ideals, how scientists should act in their work and vis-à-vis other scientists" (Zuckerman 1988, 515). So even if these ideals are entrenched in scientific practice, we should not expect them to be reflected at all times in the behavior of scientists. Of course, behavior conforming to the ideals need not indicate commitment to them either, rather than, say, self-interest. Scientists might monitor their colleagues' contributions, for example, not because the norm of disinterestedness requires it but because the scientists depend on those contributions for their own work (see Latour and Woolgar 1979, 207). Moreover, entrenchment is also expressed in other ways than by behavior conforming to the ideals—for example, by guilt when a scientist fails to conform to the ideals or by indignation when a scientist witnesses other scientists failing to conform to them. And the varieties of behavior that signify commitment to the ideals can vary from one context to another (see, e.g., Mulkay 1980).

Granting the above, historical and sociological research starting in the 1950s still failed to confirm the existence of a Mertonian ethos (see, e.g., Barnes and Dolby 1970; Mitroff 1974; Mulkay 1976; Reskin 1976; Long, Allison, and McGinness 1979; and McGinness, Allison, and Long 1982). Thus, sociologist Michael Mulkay concluded in 1976 that "detailed study by historians and sociologists has shown that in practice scientists deviate from some at least of these putative norms with a frequency which is remarkable if we presume that the latter are firmly institutionalized" (Mulkay 1976, 638–639).

By 1988, even Harriet Zuckerman, member of Merton's "Columbia School" of sociologists and supporter of its pro-science (science-is-a-relatively-just-institution-that-functions-as-it-should) outlook, expressed deep reservations. Systematic empirical studies of individual scientists' attitudes and behavior had by then, she said, provided only "sketchy" evidence for Mertonian norms— showing, for example, considerable variation in attitudes toward the norms among scientists in different disciplines and types of universities and between academic scientists and industrial scientists, and showing scientists' commit- ments to certain Mertonian norms but not to others or to both Mertonian norms and also other norms opposing them (Zuckerman 1988, 517–518). Empirical studies of scientists' commitments in the aggregate also furnished only sketchy evidence. "The available data show variability in the extent and depth of commitment to the norms, but in the absence of good measures and good samples, firm conclusions would be premature" (Zuckerman 1988, 518). For example:

> Many studies examine the extent to which universalism and particularism obtain in allocating rewards to scientists for their work. Universalism dictates that scientific merit and the quality of role performance be the sole basis for decisions on appointments, promotions, fellowships, publication, proposals for research funds, and honors. Particularism, in contrast, takes personal relations, social origins, and social statuses as the basis of such decisions [e.g., having a degree from a prestigious university, having powerful sponsors, being male rather than female]. The studies show that in practice, processes of allocation are neither wholly universalistic nor wholly particularistic. . . .
> All these studies of scientists' behavior in the aggregate imply that the ethos is neither consistently honored nor consistently flouted. (Zuckerman 1988, 518–519)

Even more disturbing, "there is no evidence, pro or con" to indicate whether a Mertonian ethos advances scientific knowledge—"to indicate whether major contributors to scientific knowledge are also more com- mitted to the ethos and conform to it more assiduously than others," for example, or to indicate whether (in Merton's words) the "ratio of scien- tific achievement to scientific potentialities" is greater in societies that permit conformity to the ethos than in those that do not (Zuckerman 1988, 519). The conclusion? For Zuckerman in 1988, it was that still more research needed to be done. For others, however, it was far more negative. Proclaimed anthropologist David Hess less than 10 years later: "For decades the consensus among social scientists has been that, as descrip- tions of the norms that actually guide scientists' action, Merton's norms do not exist in any pervasive form. Particularistic norms and values of all sorts play an important part in the de facto evaluation process in science" (Hess 1997, 57).

The first empirical claim underwriting the sociological and economic challenges to societal interference with science—the claim that a Mertonian ethos of science is entrenched in scientific practice and facilitates scientific progress—is, then, highly questionable. What of the second—that scientific progress leads to technological innovation and development? This claim, too, is questionable. True, scientific breakthroughs in basic research do sometimes fuel technological innovation. A particularly impressive example is the Nobel Prize-winning work of Charles Townes, Nikolay Basov, and Aleksandr Prokhorov on the theory of lasers that generated a vast array of unanticipated technological developments, from optic surgery and navigational instruments to military applications in outer space (Rosenberg 1986). But the transfer from basic research to technology is by no means as automatic as our challenges' second empirical claim suggests. This was made quite clear to U.S. lawmakers in the 1970s when the nation's general postwar economic prosperity, particularly in high-technology sectors, took a sharp downturn even as the funding and successes in basic research soared. Legislation followed creating both economic incentives for researchers to engage in technologically productive research and organizations (such as the Office of Technology Transfer at the National Institutes of Health) to assist in implementing these incentives—for example, to assist researchers in patenting and marketing their discoveries and inventions (and thus began what has come to be called the "commercialization" of science) (Guston 2000). But the lack of an automatic transfer from basic research to technology was clear to historians and sociologists much earlier. Indeed, historian of science Derek de Solla Price documented it in the 1960s using a statistical historiographical analysis of the relations between scientific and technological literatures and the communities that produce them. What he found was insularity and parallel development rather than interaction and cognitive exchange: "the cumulating bodies of science and of technology are each available quite readily to the other at a distance from their respective research front equal to about one generation of students" (D. de S. Price 1965, 564). "It is therefore naive," he concluded, "to regard technology as applied science. . . . Because of this one should beware of any claims that particular scientific research is needed for particular technological potentials" (568). Much the same conclusion was suggested by the U.S. Defense Department's 1960s "Project Hindsight" retrospective study of the contributions of scientific research to continuing improvements in military technology.

> Of the several hundred critical "events" in the development of twenty weapons systems, fewer than 1 in 10 could be traced to research of any kind and fewer than 1 in 100 to basic research untargeted on defense needs. Most improvements in this weaponry were found to be modifications of existing technology or the result of development activities inspired not by research but by an awareness of the technical limitations of existing systems. (Stokes 1997, 55)

This example is entirely typical: "Most innovation is done with the available knowledge already in the heads of the people in the organization doing the work"—knowledge that includes, of course, already established scientific as well as technological information—"and, to a lesser extent, with other information readily accessible to them. It is only when those sources of information fall short of solving the problem that there is a need for research in order to complete a given innovation" (Kline and Rosenberg 1986, 288).

If the relation between basic research and technological innovation is not as simple and direct as our challenges' second empirical claim suggests, however, neither is it as unidirectional. Indeed, technological innovation fuels basic research at least as frequently as basic research fuels technological innovation. This is especially true of many of the instruments, materials, and processes utilized in basic research (think of how the invention of the telescope led to Galileo's and others' cosmological breakthroughs), but it is true in other kinds of cases as well. For example, basic research is sometimes motivated and structured by technological needs and developments (as in the case of Sadi Carnot's endeavors to increase the efficiency of the early steam engine, which resulted in his founding contribution to the science of thermodynamics), and basic research sometimes takes as its subject matter the materials and processes unveiled by technological developments (as in the case of Irving Langmuir's Nobel Prize-winning research working out the physics of the surfaces of the devices being produced by General Electric and the other electronics firms of his day, which cleared the way for further advances in that technology). Sometimes, as well, basic research and applied research are simply conducted together (as in the case of Louis Pasteur, who strove to understand at the most fundamental level the process of disease as well as the other microbiological processes he discovered at the same time that he strove to deal with anthrax in sheep and cattle; cholera in chickens; spoilage in milk, wine, and vinegar; and rabies in people). (See, for discussions of the Carnot, Langmuir, and Pasteur examples, Stokes 1997). What all of this shows is not only that the sociological and economic challenges' second empirical claim—that scientific progress leads to technological innovation and development—is simplistic but even that the concepts it is based on—that basic research is performed without thought of practical ends, that only it, and not applied research or technology, results in general knowledge and an understanding of nature, that there is an inherent tension between the drive toward fundamental understanding, on the one hand, and considerations of use, on the other, and hence, a radical separation between basic research and applied research/technology, and so on—these concepts are simplistic, too.[7]

What, then, of the third empirical claim underwriting the sociological and economic challenges to societal interference with science—that technological innovation and development lead to the kinds of social benefits demanded by the ideal of socially responsible science? This, too, is simplistic.

7. Some have therefore suggested new concepts such as technoscience to replace them. See, for example, Latour 1987, 174.

True, technological innovation and development, with or without the aid of basic research, have yielded or helped to yield such things as food in greater variety and abundance, produced more quickly and efficiently; the near eradication of such dreaded diseases as scarlet fever, smallpox, leprosy, and polio and impressive progress on other diseases such as HIV/AIDS; better-insulated, more comfortable homes, with more conveniences, produced more quickly and efficiently; more sophisticated communications systems; and quicker, more convenient modes of transportation. But technological innovation and development, with or without the aid of basic research, have also yielded or helped to yield such things as a food supply tainted with every manner of pesticides, herbicides, antibiotics, growth hormones, and other harmful chemicals; polluted air and water and a depleted ozone layer; ever-rising mountains of garbage and toxic wastes; ever more prevalent heart disease and strokes, cancer, diabetes, gallbladder disease, and other dreaded diseases related to overadequate (overfatty, over-protein-filled, over-calorie-filled) diets and polluted environments; ever more depleted supplies of the world's resources and widespread extinction of plant and animal life; and, of course, enormous stockpiles of nuclear and other weapons. These "social benefits," in turn, have exacerbated social inequalities. Wealthier individuals, for example, a goodly proportion of whom are white, can afford to buy bottled water and better, safer (e.g., organic) food, can purchase the most up-to-date medical services and treatments to deal with cancer and heart disease, can move away from degraded and contaminated areas, can more easily cope with environmental disasters, and can access more and better information about their choices. Poorer individuals—and countries—have far fewer of these options. Technological innovation and development may even *produce* the inequalities:

> The experience of the past 30 or more years shows that the phenomenon of science-and-technology-based economic growth seems to be accompanied by increasing inequality in distribution of economic benefits. . . . This inequality appears on numerous fronts, including high unemployment and underemployment rates [perhaps in part a result of higher productivity], persistent levels of poverty, and soaring concentration of wealth, each of which are apparent both within nations and between nations on a global basis, even as global wealth continues to grow. (Sarewitz, Foladori, Invernizzi, and Garfinkel 2004, 69)

And there is every reason to believe that the inequalities produced or exacerbated by science and technology will continue to increase. Think, for example, of the steroids and other athletic performance enhancers now available to wealthier individuals, as well as the other enhancers now on the horizon—the nano-scale implantable memory enhancers, the nano-scale implantable sensors and associated medical devices to monitor and respond to health problems, the germline gene therapies to create "designer" children, and the like—enhancers that will make it possible for the already advantaged to become even more advantaged. Far from advances in science and technology making the ideal of socially responsible science unnecessary—by automatically leading to the social benefits demanded by that ideal—just the opposite seems to be the case: scientific and technological advances now threaten to make the ideal of socially responsible science even more necessary.

THE POLITICAL CHALLENGE

The empirical claims underwriting the sociological and economic challenges to societal interference with science—that a Mertonian ethos of science is entrenched in scientific practice and facilitates scientific progress, that scientific progress leads to technological innovation and development, and that technological innovation and development lead to the kinds of social benefits demanded by the ideal of socially responsible science—these empirical claims are all, then, problematic. The sociological and economic challenges have not, therefore, succeeded in showing that the ideal of socially responsible science is unnecessary. Nor, as we have already seen, have the epistemological and historical challenges succeeded in showing that the ideal of socially responsible science is epistemically unacceptable. But is the ideal of socially responsible science *politically* unacceptable?

Many now claim, after all, that interference with the conduct of scientific research violates scientists' rights. According to Article 13 of the Charter of Fundamental Rights of the European Union, for example: "The arts and scientific research shall be free of constraint. Academic freedom shall be respected" (European Union 2000, 11); and many countries' constitutions acknowledge the same fundamental right—for example, Article 5 of the German Constitution ("art and science, research and teaching are free") and Article 33 of the Italian Constitution ("the arts and sciences as well as their teaching are free") (Santosuosso, Fabio, and Sellaroli 2007, 275). The Declaration of the 2006 World Congress for Freedom of Scientific Research adds that "freedom of scientific research is required by democracy," "because all democracies are founded upon the value of the individual, individual choice and upon the premise that one of the first and most important functions of democratic government is to preserve and promote the liberty of citizens and to do no harm." The Declaration also proclaims that freedom of scientific research "is a basic civil and political right," "because it is a dimension of freedom of thought and freedom of speech" "and is one of the main guarantors of human health and welfare" (Lalli and Sorrentino 2007, 333). The American journal *Progress in Physics* 2006 Declaration of Academic Freedom (Scientific Human Rights) further elaborates: "scientific creation is a human right no less than other such rights . . . as propounded in international covenants and international law," and hence "scientific research must be free of the latent and overt repressive influence of bureaucratic, political, religious and pecuniary directives" (Rabounski 2006, 57). More particularly:

Fundamental Rights of the European Union, for example, was drafted by a convention of 62 individuals representing heads of state and government, the president of the European Commission, the European Parliament, and the national parliaments. All of the meetings of this convention and all of the documents it produced were made public, and the convention also organized public hearings and analyzed position papers from nongovernmental organizations representing varied interests (churches and confessional groups; human-rights defense leagues; property owners; trade unions; business undertakings; asylum seekers; associations defending the interests of women, children, gays, and lesbians; environmental protection groups; etc.). Furthermore, the Charter was ratified by all 25 member states of the European Union (European Union n.d.). For all of its thoroughness and democratic intent, however, the convention apparently never solicited input from scientists. By contrast, the 2006 World Congress for Freedom of Scientific Research issued its declaration of rights as a result of sessions participated in by university scientists and directors of research institutes from around the world, as well as bioethicists, political scientists, members of national judiciaries, international patient-advocacy groups, representatives from national and regional governments, and legislators from national parliaments. Congress sessions were again open to the public, and all contributions were published on the Internet. And future congresses will continue these procedures (see Associazione Lucacoscioni 2005, Lalli and Sorrentino 2007, and World Congress for Freedom of Scientific Research 2009). Still, the focus was on biomedical researchers and the biomedical sciences and issues such as limitations on the funding of stem-cell research. The most detailed and comprehensive of the above declarations' characterizations of scientists' rights, on the other hand—the Declaration of Academic Freedom—was produced by only one scientist, the editor-in-chief of *Progress in Physics*, himself a physicist, and was motivated primarily by issues of special concern to academic scientists. Still, it was published online in seven different languages (English, Spanish, Dutch, Bulgarian, Romanian, French, and Russian) as an open letter to all scientists (see Rabounski 2006). If the ideal of socially responsible science aspires to function in ways similar to the above declarations, though in ways relevant to all scientists, not just biomedical researchers or academic scientists, what procedures for establishing scientists' rights and the needs that constrain those rights will it have to employ?

Third, what concrete results can we expect to follow from the ideal of socially responsible science? Regarding the Charter of Fundamental Rights of the European Union, its aim is to enable citizens more effectively to defend themselves against violations of their rights by providing citizens with more explicit (and accessible) information about those rights and by providing judges with more explicit guidance in their reading of those rights. And given the legal systems already in place in both the European Union and its member states, the Charter gives definite hope of fulfilling its aim in most cases, though only time will tell how any of this will affect the conduct of science. For its part, the Declaration of the 2006 World Congress for Freedom of Scientific Research has invited participants to join in drafting the "Statute of the World Congress in order to identify jointly issues, objectives and specific responsibilities in the respective fields of research or at the respective regional levels" (Lalli and Sorrentino 2007, 335). And the Declaration of Academic Freedom calls for "all supporting scientists" to "abide by this Declaration, as an indication of solidarity with the concerned international scientific community, and to vouchsafe the rights of the citizenry of the world to unfettered scientific creation according to their individual skills and disposition, for the advancement of science and, to their utmost ability as decent citizens in an indecent world, the benefit of Mankind" (Rabounski 2006, 57). But again, only time will tell how any of this will affect the conduct of science. If the ideal of socially responsible science seeks to impose constraints on scientific research similar to those suggested by the above declarations, how can it still ensure more concrete results than these?

Finally, what role might philosophers of science—a group prominent in its total absence from all of the meetings and hearings and position papers and deliberations leading to the above declarations—what role might philosophers of science play in articulating the ideal of socially responsible science and dealing with the above set of issues?

It is to these most fundamental questions that we now finally turn.

5

The Prospects for Philosophy of Science in the Twenty-First Century

A promise was made at the outset of this book to provide you with a new program of research for philosophy of science. Has the promise been kept? Let's take stock.

Chapter 1 began with a review of some of the most pressing problems women confront in society today—problems such as job and wage discrimination, violence against women, and the "vanishing" and trafficking of females—and went on to illustrate ways in which science (e.g., psychology and biology and archaeology and economics and medical research) has both perpetuated and added to these problems. There followed a selection of normative questions regarding the social responsibility of science (SRS questions). For example, should science prioritize research that promises support for egalitarian views and programs and deprioritize research that threatens such views and programs? Should science adopt modes of evaluation of research that favor egalitarian views? Should science adopt a robust affirmative-action policy for women (or for feminists or for diversity)? And so on. These questions were noteworthy because they dealt with standard philosophy of science fare—research pursuit and evaluation and the ultimate goals of science, what makes for scientific objectivity and what threatens it—but at the same time went beyond standard fare. That is, they dealt with the social effects of science as well as its epistemic features, the social conditions (e.g., funding priorities or staffing policies) that encourage science to have those features and effects, the need for social/scientific change, and the social/political/epistemic initiatives needed to bring about that change. But did they define a new *program* for philosophy of science? They dealt, after all, only with a limited range of issues, ones concerning women and their quest for equality. Still, these SRS questions had analogues concerning race and ethnicity, sexual orientation, and disability, even the environment and world peace. Or so it was claimed.

Next, chapter 2 explored the twentieth-century roots of current philosophy of science and its penchant for dealing with science as if science existed in a (social, political, economic . . .) vacuum. Of course, chapter 2 uncovered no defensible reasons, epistemic or otherwise, to indulge this penchant and many reasons not to. It also uncovered, in the early-twentieth-century work of the Vienna Circle, an important historical precedent for doing philosophy of science in a more "contextualized" way—one that located science within its wider societal context—and the valuable contributions, both philosophical and political, that could generate. A contemporary program for a contextualized philosophy of science inspired by the work of feminists could therefore be an attractive option.

Chapter 3 thus took up the SRS questions posed in chapter 1. This is the project feminist philosophers of science, as well as feminist historians and sociologists of science and feminist scientists themselves, have been working on for more than three decades now, and the project has generated a number of very different kinds of responses. The methodological approach and the ideal of value-free science, the social approach and the social value management ideal of science, and the naturalist approach and the empiricist ideal of science were all considered, but in the end, a new approach was found necessary. This was the political approach, with its ideal of socially responsible science. According to this approach, sound social values as well as sound epistemic values must control every aspect of the scientific research process, from the choice of research questions to the communication and application of results, this to be enforced by such political means as funding requirements on research. This approach certainly promised to do away with the problems of androcentrism and sexism in science illustrated in chapter 1. Nonetheless, its method of doing so—by deliberately and explicitly politicizing science—evokes much apprehension and critique.

Chapter 4, therefore, defended the political approach with its ideal of socially responsible science against five important challenges: the epistemological challenge, the historical challenge, the sociological challenge, the economic challenge, and the political challenge. Even so, fundamental questions remained. In particular, how can the political approach's ideal of socially responsible science be spelled out so that it is at once (1) comprehensive enough to apply to all scientific fields and practitioners but also (2) specific enough and perspicuous enough to be capable of yielding the desired concrete results and (3) warranted enough to command the respect and adherence of scientists from different cultures, religious traditions, and economic and political systems and levels of development? Moreover, (4) what role might philosophers of science play in such a venture? If the ideal of socially responsible science is to be a serious proposal, these fundamental questions must be broached. What headway can we make on these daunting questions here?

A GLANCE, AGAIN, AT THE PAST

Recall the terrain explored in chapter 2—how philosophy of science had both come into its own and not come into its own by the middle of the twentieth century. On the one hand, philosophy of science by mid-century enjoyed increasing prestige within philosophy and science studies circles, due at least in part to the ambitious goal philosophy of science had adopted: to articulate and even improve upon what lay at the very heart of science's success, scientific rationality itself. On the other hand, philosophy of science's mode of pursuing this goal left something to be desired. Indeed, as we saw in chapter 2, at mid-century only the logical aspects of science were thought relevant to scientific rationality—only those logical aspects, in fact, related to Hans Reichenbach's context of justification. Articulating and improving upon scientific rationality meant reconstructing science using the modes of conceptualization provided by formal logic and empiricist epistemology—reconstructing science in such a way as to maximize the virtues considered essential to those modes of conceptualization. Thus, scientific theories were represented as axiom systems partially interpreted by an observational language itself interpreted on the basis of observation. Explanations invoking such theories were represented as the logical derivation of the statements to be explained (the "explananda") from the theories and statements of initial conditions (the "explanans"). The assessment of these theories was represented as the logical derivation of observation statements ("predictions") from the theories (in conjunction with statements of initial conditions) and the comparison of those predictions with statements describing the results of observation or experiment. And so on. But, as Thomas Kuhn, Paul Feyerabend, Imre Lakatos, Stephen Toulmin, and a host of others made especially clear, those logical aspects of science, though they were surely relevant to an understanding of scientific rationality, were far from the whole story. Indeed, the critics suggested that those logical aspects provided very little of the story—that what philosophy of science was offering as an account of scientific rationality was of surprisingly little relevance to actual science.

No matter. By the end of the twentieth century, as we saw, the mid-century critics and those they influenced had more than compensated for the first lean offerings of professional philosophy of science. No longer was scientific rationality thought to be confined merely to Reichenbach's context of justification; it was now understood to encompass as well the abductive and other reasoning processes that populated his context of discovery. Nor was scientific rationality confined any longer to logic, whether of discovery or justification. Indeed, social factors, such as competition and cooperation among scientists, and particular patterns of consensus and dissensus, were found to contribute to scientific success, and it became possible to speak of the rationality of various modes of community organization and community practice as well as the rationality of various modes of individual behavior. Even the more material aspects of science, such as scientific instrumentation and scientific modeling, were found to relate to scientific rationality, since they embedded within them scientific knowledge and thereby contributed to the development of new knowledge. And the old questions of theory structure and theory validation were treated in new ways, ways that were informed by historical accounts of the temporally extended research programs that generated such theories and determined the conditions of their acceptance or rejection. By the end of the twentieth century, in short, articulating and improving upon scientific rationality was found to require involvement with a great many aspects of science, historical, social, and material as well as logical, and the resources from a variety of fields—including the history of science, the sociology of science, cognitive science, social epistemology, and the history of technology—were required to do this well. But by century's end, articulating and improving upon scientific rationality was not found to require involvement with the *ethical* aspects of science, and hence, no resources from such fields as ethics or political philosophy or public policy were required to do philosophy of science well. True, feminist philosophers of science, as we saw in chapter 3, were speaking a great deal about the social values in science and how they relate to scientific rationality, and philosophers of biology were occasionally taking up such topics as the ethical implications of the genome project or the status of creation science or the political as well as conceptual and empirical problems associated with sociobiology. But for the rest, to quote from a 1996 essay by Philip Kitcher and Nancy Cartwright, the ethics of science was "virtually unexplored territory" (Kitcher and Cartwright 1996, 149). This, of course, tied in with the general failure to contextualize philosophy of science discussed in chapter 2.

Meanwhile, in the sciences—that which philosophy of science was supposed to be about—new or newly revised ethical codes were proliferating by century's end. On the American scene, the American Physical Society adopted its Guidelines for Professional Conduct in 1991 (updated and expanded in 2002), the American Chemical Society adopted The Chemist's Code of Conduct in 1994, the Society for American Archaeology adopted the Principles of Archaeological Ethics in 1996, the American Sociological Association approved its revised Code of Ethics and Policies and Procedures in 1997, the American Society for Biochemistry and Molecular Biology approved its Code of Ethics in 1998, and the American Psychological Association adopted the most recent version of its Ethical Principles of Psychologists and Code of Conduct in 2002, to cite just a few examples. On the international scene, there were, for example, the Uppsala Code of Ethics for Scientists published in 1984 and considered a basis for later international guidelines; The Toronto Resolution of 1991, whose purpose was to create a common moral framework worldwide for the conduct of research; and the Code of Conduct for Scientists called for by the 1999 World Conference on Science organized by UNESCO and the International Council for Science, work toward which began appearing in 2001. All of these codes acknowledged scientists' multiple responsibilities—for example, to their individual disciplines and to science in general; to society and the environment; to their employers, employees, coworkers, and students; and to their human, animate, and

Or consider another part of the Chemist's Code of Conduct and another motivation for at least some of the new ethics codes at century's end. Concern over global problems—concern over ever mounting threats to the environment, ever mounting threats to public health, ever mounting threats to world peace—concern over these problems also played a role in the appearance of some of the ethics codes. The expectation had always been that science would solve such problems, but by the end of the twentieth century there was a growing sense that science had failed to solve them and may even have made them worse.[1] As one of the background papers for the 1999 World Conference on Science, the conference that was to produce a new international code of ethics for scientists, proclaimed:

> Today . . . science suffers from a serious image problem. In large parts of the world, people no longer conceive of science as being essentially a benefactor of humanity, nor do they readily associate science with the classical quest to develop a more enlightened civilization. Trust in the ethical integrity and responsibility of scientists is declining partly to be replaced by suspicion and fear of abuses of various kinds. . . . The present state of affairs calls for a powerful statement about the ethical responsibilities of science towards society and present or future generations, and towards the environment. (International Council for Science's Standing Committee on Responsibility and Ethics in Science 1999)

But all that the Chemist's Code of Conduct (American Chemical Society 1994) says about the ethical responsibilities of chemistry to society and present and future generations is: "Chemists have a professional responsibility to serve the public interest and welfare and to further knowledge of science. Chemists should actively be concerned with the health and welfare of co-workers, consumers and the community. Public comments on scientific matters should be made with care and precision, without unsubstantiated, exaggerated, or premature statements." And all that the Chemist's Code of Conduct says about the ethical responsibilities of chemistry to the environment is: "Chemists should understand and anticipate the environmental consequences of their work. Chemists have responsibility to avoid pollution and to protect the environment." But the Code leaves completely undefined what all these responsibilities amount to, these responsibilities to serve the public interest and welfare, avoid pollution, and protect the environment, and it is important to remember that the Chemist's Code also covers the ethical responsibilities of chemists to their employers—who, of course, include, among others, manufacturers of petrochemicals and the pharmaceutical industry. These responsibilities to

---

1. Global warming formed a particularly painful example. During the last decade of the twentieth century and the first few years of the twenty-first, the United States spent upwards of $25 billion on global-climate-system research as a basis for creating appropriate climate policy, but it has yet to take any meaningful action on such policy (Sarewitz 2006). The problem, meanwhile, keeps getting worse.

employers read: "Chemists should promote and protect the legitimate interests of their employers, perform work honestly and competently, fulfill obligations, and safeguard proprietary information."

Other ethical codes within the sciences have comparable problems. The American Physical Society's Guidelines for Professional Conduct (2002), for example, though far more precise in dealing with the issues of gift authorship and other kinds of scientific misconduct, never even mentions physicists' responsibilities to society or future generations or the environment or even physicists' responsibilities to their employers, many of whom, of course, are involved in the development and deployment of military weaponry. In fact, the only responsibility of physicists noted in their code is their responsibility to *science*, physics in particular:

> The Constitution of the American Physical Society states that the objective of the Society shall be the advancement and diffusion of the knowledge of physics. It is the purpose of this statement to advance that objective by presenting ethical guidelines for Society members.
>
> Each physicist is a citizen of the community of science. Each shares responsibility for the welfare of this community. Science is best advanced when there is mutual trust, based upon honest behavior, throughout the community. Acts of deception, or any other acts that deliberately compromise the advancement of science, are unacceptable.

The Code of Ethics of the American Society for Biochemistry and Molecular Biology (1998), on the other hand, does acknowledge other responsibilities besides the responsibility to science—for example, the responsibility to the public "to promote and follow practices that enhance the public interest or well-being" and the responsibility to trainees "to create and maintain a working environment that encourages cultural diversity." These responsibilities are, again, unhelpfully vague, but the inclusion of the responsibility to encourage cultural diversity is still noteworthy. Or rather, its absence from other ethics codes is noteworthy given the prominence accorded the lack of diversity in the sciences at century's end. Indeed, neither the Chemist's Code of Conduct nor the American Physical Society's Guidelines for Professional Conduct nor the American Society for Microbiology's Code of Ethics (2005) nor many other ethics codes even mention diversity. Of course, the Ethics Statement of the American Institute of Biological Sciences (2002) does acknowledge a responsibility for diversity, though not so much a responsibility to encourage diversity as not to stamp it out: "Be civil and respectful in professional interactions, avoiding discrimination, based on race, gender, sexual orientation, religion, or age. Treat colleagues, students, and employees fairly." But the Ethics Statement at the same time lacks any acknowledgment of other important responsibilities—for example, to society or employers or the environment. The deficiencies go on and on.

True, by century's end, many scientific societies were engaging in other activities besides the formulation of ethics codes to help educate members about their responsibilities as scientists. These activities included arranging programs and lectures on research ethics at annual or regional meetings, creating ethics committees to advise and/or conduct investigations of misconduct allegations and plan societies' ethics agendas, publishing columns or articles on research ethics in professional journals and newsletters as well as supporting other kinds of publications on research ethics, posting resource materials on Web sites, organizing mentorship programs or special activities for students and trainees, and presenting awards to members exemplifying integrity in research. Indeed, a survey of scientific societies conducted in 1999–2000 by the American Association for the Advancement of Science (AAAS) Program on Scientific Freedom, Responsibility and Law found that just over half (52%) of the societies surveyed indicated that they were currently engaging in or planned to engage in at least one of these types of activities, and 19% indicated that they sponsored five or more of these types of activities. Unfortunately, the AAAS study also found that the societies "lack rigorous assessment methods [regarding the effectiveness of these activities] and, in some cases, even an understanding of how they might conduct useful evaluations." As a result: "Although many of the societies we surveyed are willing to expend effort and resources to promote research integrity through codes and activities, they are not engaging in any systematic assessment of the effectiveness of these efforts" and hence "have little idea of whether those efforts have had any impact on their members' knowledge, attitudes, and behavior" and how those efforts might be improved (Iverson, Frankel, and Siang 2003, 150–151). Meanwhile, another 2000 study— this time conducted by representatives of the American Psychological Association but presented at the same AAAS/Office of Research Integrity meeting on "The Role and Activities of Scientific Societies in Promoting Research Integrity"—"examined the ethics principles and codes of a wide variety of scientific associations, spanning the gamut of scientific disciplines," in order "to raise questions about the purpose and value of scientific associations' efforts to monitor and regulate the ethical conduct of their membership so as to promote integrity in research" (Bullock and Panicker 2003, 160). This second study suggested that

> If a professional code is intended to be *enforceable*, it should include procedures for handling allegations of misconduct or unethical behavior. This might be at the association level if the organization has the necessary resources to ensure adequate adjudication (due process), or it might be to specify other organizations with relevant authority, such as universities or governmental agencies. (167)

But the study found that "only a relatively small number of associations supplement their ethics codes with detailed reporting or grievance procedures, provide information about procedures for handling allegations of misconduct or unethical behavior, or specify sanctions against those who violate the code" (165). The upshot is that by the year 2000, little could be offered in the way of success stories for "scientific associations' efforts to monitor and regulate," whether through educational programs or through enforcement mechanisms, "the ethical conduct of their membership so as to promote integrity in research." Small wonder the U.S. government had already (in 1993) authorized a new Office of Research Integrity (ORI), the cosponsor of the 2000 meeting at which the results of both of the above studies were presented, to oversee universities in their management of research integrity, conduct its own investigations when necessary, and engage in outreach and educational efforts (see, e.g., Guston 2000).

Yet even with government intervention (in the United States and elsewhere), the problems that motivated the ethics codes continue.

Indeed, the parade of national and international scandals continues. Examples include the fabrication of data at Bell Laboratories and Lawrence Berkeley National Laboratory in 2002; the suppression of data regarding Vioxx by Merck researchers in the United States and Actonel by Proctor and Gamble researchers in the United Kingdom in 2005; the imprisonment in 2006 of American clinical researcher Eric Poehlman for the fabrication of more than a decade's worth of scientific data on obesity, menopause, and aging, data that were used to obtain millions of dollars in federal grants from the National Institutes of Health; the indictment in 2006 of Korean stem-cell pioneer Woo Suk Hwang on charges of fraud, embezzlement (of $2.99 million in state funds and private donations), and violations of bioethics law (see, e.g., Brumfiel 2002; Johnson 2002; Langreth and Herper 2005; Baty 2005; Interlandi 2006; Wohn and Normile 2006). The less public cases of fraud and other sorts of scientific misconduct also continue, reported in articles and books such as *The Great Betrayal: Fraud in Science*, by science journalist Horace Freeland Judson (2004); "Scientists Behaving Badly," by social scientists Brian Martinson, Melissa Anderson, and Raymond De Vries (2005); *Fraud and Misconduct in Biomedical Research*, edited by cofounder of MedicoLegal Investigations Frank Wells and Vice Chancellor of the University of Sussex Michael Farthing (2008); and *Bending Science: How Special Interests Corrupt Public Health Research*, by University of Texas law professors Thomas McGarity and Wendy Wagner (2008).

Fear of what science is unleashing on society continues as well—fear of genetically modified foods, for example, and foods laced with pesticides, growth hormones, and antibiotics (that lead, among other things, to antibiotic-resistant strains of disease); fear of the effects of the more than 500 new chemicals released every year into the environment; fear of the possible future reproductive cloning of humans; fear of possible nuclear, chemical, or biological terrorism. And, of course, mistrust of science continues, typified by the widespread use of alternative medicine ("the total annual cost of alternative medicine in the United States exceeds $27 billion, comparable to the total cost of standard medicine;" Agin 2006, 114), the widespread interest in organic farming, and the widespread adoption of creation science and intelligent design.

Finally, lack of diversity in science and lack of equal opportunities in science for women and underrepresented minority men also continue. Indeed, recent reports by the National Academy of Sciences/National Academy of Engineering/Institute of Medicine (Committee on Maximizing the Potential of Women 2007), the Barnard Center for Research on Women (Wylie, Jakobsen, and Fosado 2007), the National Science Foundation (Committee on Equal Opportunities 2007), the Diversity in Science Association (Nelson 2007), and the American Association of University Professors (West and Curtis 2006)—recent reports by these organizations use the results of research in social psychology, cognitive science, sociology, and economics to reveal the factors that systematically disadvantage women and minority men in science (factors such as inhospitable workplace environments, institutional structures, and work patterns and biased modes of evaluation and systems of reward).

At the same time, however, the development of the wherewithal to address all of these problems also continues. Indeed, many of the same reports that expose the problems also offer solutions. For example, in *Bending Science*, McGarity and Wagner (2008) propose new legally enforceable information-disclosure requirements (e.g., regarding negative outcomes of studies and conflicts of interest) so that scientists, journalists, public-interest groups, and even the general public will be able more easily to assess scientific research, especially research that is relevant to public policy. McGarity and Wagner also offer ways to improve government peer-review processes that oversee policy-relevant research and also explain the conditions under which independent science advisory panels of experts should be convened (and how they should be convened) to review specific bodies of such science. The National Academy of Sciences/National Academy of Engineering/Institute of Medicine's report *Beyond Bias and Barriers: Fulfilling the Potential of Women in Academic Science and Engineering* (Committee on Maximizing the Potential of Women 2007) details actions that individual institutions have taken to improve the hiring, retention, and advancement of women science faculty and the flourishing of women science students, and it offers suggestions for extending these activities across higher education (even giving a scorecard for continuous assessment of institutional efforts and suggestions for appropriate sanctions for noncompliance). And books and journal articles such as *Green Chemistry: Theory and Practice* by Paul Anastas and John Warner (1998) and *Science*'s special 2002 issue on green chemistry respond to the public's concerns over the effects of science on society and the environment with blueprints for change. Thus, according to the introduction to the special *Science* issue:

> Few people choose to live without the benefits of modern chemistry, but often the benefits are associated with other fields, such as medicine, materials, or engineering. Chemistry is more often associated in the public mind with pollution. . . . Many

chemical industry processes have been or still are highly polluting; for example, by emitting persistent pollutants that could interfere with the hormonal messenger system in aquatic animals and in humans. Organic solvents are particularly problematic, because many are toxic and are not broken down easily in the environment. Waste is another major issue.[2] . . . Over recent decades, the chemical industry has been increasingly regulated in order to reduce harmful emissions and effluents and ensure worker safety. . . . Now scientists are calling for an integrated approach that goes beyond regulation of individual chemicals. Green chemistry focuses instead on making whole chemical processes less wasteful and damaging to the environment. (Fahrenkamp-Uppenbrink 2002, 798)

Anastas and Warner, in fact, offer 12 "principles of green chemistry" to reduce or eliminate the generation or use of hazardous substances in the design, manufacture, and application of chemical products. They include:

- Prevent waste: Design chemical syntheses to prevent waste, leaving no waste to treat or clean up.
- Use renewable feedstocks: Use raw materials and feedstocks that are renewable rather than depleting. Renewable feedstocks are often made from agricultural products or are the wastes of other processes; depleting feedstocks are made from fossil fuels (petroleum, natural gas, or coal) or are mined.
- Use safer solvents and reaction conditions: Avoid using solvents, separation agents, or other auxiliary chemicals. If these chemicals are necessary, use innocuous chemicals.
- Design chemicals and products to degrade after use: Design chemical products to break down to innocuous substances after use so that they do not accumulate in the environment.

And awards such as the U.S. Presidential Green Chemistry Challenge Awards, the Canadian Green Chemistry Medal, and the European Green and Sustainable Chemistry Awards have been created to encourage the implementation of these principles (Jensen 2001; Royal Society of Chemistry 2006; U.S. Environmental Protection Agency 2008).

All of these requirements and procedures and principles not only point to solutions to the problems motivating the ethics codes in the sciences; they also point to more adequate ethics codes, codes that specify more well-defined, more defensible goals for science (regarding, e.g., the protection of the environment or the promotion of diversity among scientists) and clearer, more concrete ways to meet these goals. The requirements and procedures and principles referred to above thus suggest that the project of formulating adequate ethics codes is doable. But they also suggest that the project of formulating adequate ethics codes is important. Indeed, the above-mentioned requirements and procedures and

2. "On a waste-to-product ratio, the pharmaceutical industry is one of the least environmentally acceptable, generating 25 to 100 pounds of waste for every pound of active pharmaceutical ingredient manufactured. As much as 80% of that waste is solvent" (Hoag 2008, 30).

principles—*legal* requirements and *university* procedures and chemical principles designed to replace *government regulations*—clearly show that if the scientific community fails to regulate its own activities, other bodies will. And this latter alternative is by far the less attractive one—for science *and* society—for a number of reasons.

To begin with, scientists have traditionally been reluctant to be regulated by outsiders, and outsiders, for their part, have been reluctant to regulate science (for examples of this, see Goodstein 1995)—due to the extent of the technical knowledge it takes to do the job well and, of course, the desire for autonomy on the part of the scientific community. Adequate ethics codes, however, would be constructed by scientists and enforced by scientists, and they could be revised (as the better ethics codes in the sciences have been repeatedly revised)[3] when conditions require it or new knowledge enables it. Adequate ethics codes, in short, would represent scientists regulating themselves, the condition generally held to be appropriate for the professions.

In addition, adequate ethics codes self-imposed by the scientific community and enforced by the scientific community would inspire public trust in science and, in fact, would earn that trust; by contrast, the need for continuing—indeed, increasing—regulation of science by external authorities can have no other effect than the erosion of public trust in science.

Finally, clear, accessible, well-publicized ethics codes with clear modes of enforcement serve important pedagogical functions. They tell scientists and students of science and others—industry and government and the public—what is legitimately expected of scientists. They can thus serve as a mechanism for holding not only scientists publicly accountable for what they do but also industry and government accountable for what they demand of scientists. Clear, accessible, well-publicized ethics codes can also themselves be the subject of public scrutiny and assessment as well as public accommodation, and can thereby provide a further measure of public accountability for science.

There is another reason the project of formulating adequate ethics codes for the sciences is important. Recall the questions with which we began: How can the political approach's ideal of socially responsible science defended in chapters 3 and 4 be spelled out so that it is at once (1) comprehensive enough to apply to all scientific fields and practitioners but also (2) specific enough and perspicuous enough to be capable of yielding the desired concrete results and (3) warranted enough to command the respect and adherence of scientists from different cultures, religious traditions, and economic and political systems and levels of development? Moreover, (4) what role might philosophers of science play in such a venture? Clear, accessible, well-publicized ethics codes for the

3. For example, the American Psychological Association's Ethical Principles of Psychologists and Code of Conduct has been revised nine times since 1953. See American Psychological Association 2002.

various sciences, adequately formulated, would be the piecemeal elaboration of the ideal of socially responsible science—comprehensive enough, when taken together, to apply to all scientific fields but also specific enough and perspicuous enough, one at a time, to yield the desired concrete results. But would such codes ever be warranted enough to command the respect and adherence of scientists all over the world in each scientific specialty? There are already international codes of ethics for some scientific specialties—for example, the International Ethical Guidelines for Biomedical Research Involving Human Subjects of the Council for International Organizations of Medical Sciences, the Code of Ethics of the International Sociological Association, and the First Code of Ethics of the World Archaeological Congress—and there is currently much interest in creating international codes for other scientific specialties and even a unified international code for all of science (see, e.g., Evers 2001). One reason for this interest is the international cooperation and collaboration now required for most scientific specialties. Another is the fear that research judged impermissible by one code of ethics in one country could simply be moved to another country with a more permissive code of ethics or no code at all, thereby undercutting the code of the first country and, ultimately, ethics codes in general. Still a third reason is the need for international efforts to deal with international problems in science such as fraud and other kinds of scientific misconduct and research aimed at or serving biological, chemical, or other kinds of terrorism. All these reasons and others besides make the possibility of adequate, well-justified, well-respected international codes of ethics for the various sciences highly plausible.

But what role could philosophers of science play in such a venture? The formulation of adequate ethics codes for the various sciences is a highly interdisciplinary, empirical project, one that requires, for each scientific specialty (e.g., chemistry), information from within that specialty (e.g., regarding its traditional disciplinary aims and the kinds of research considered valuable, provided by insiders), information about that specialty (e.g., its funding arrangements and the structural conditions that allow or encourage misconduct among its members, gathered by outsiders such as sociologists and economists), and information about the concerns of those affected by the specialty (e.g., industry, government, and the public at large, offered by a variety of observers and stakeholders such as political scientists, economists, ecologists, and environmental advocacy groups). The formulation of adequate ethics codes for the various sciences, however, is also—is first and foremost—a *normative* project, one that looks deeply into the aims and attendant responsibilities scientists *ought* to set for themselves, both individually and collectively, given the kinds of factors mentioned above. And philosophers of science have a deep grounding in normative issues and a honed facility for articulating and clarifying as well as analyzing and criticizing arguments relevant to normative issues. More significant, this normative project is an epistemic as well as an ethical project; the formulation of adequate ethics codes for the sciences is a response to needs that are simultaneously epistemic and ethical. Scientific fraud, for example, is not only unethical but also a serious threat to the validity of accepted scientific knowledge. Exclusionary practices within the scientific community—practices that exclude women and minority men from equal opportunities with white men, for example—are not only unethical—unjust—but are also epistemically damaging, since they decrease the pool of available talent and, as the work of women scientists during the last few decades amply demonstrates, also tend to leave in place the biases associated with the group that excludes. The failure of scientists to respond to the legitimate needs of society is not only unethical—an unfair recompense for the support society has lavished on science—but is also a threat to society's continued support of science as well as society's continued participation in science, and thereby to science's continued epistemic success. And so on. Helping to make the ethics codes in the sciences adequate thereby connects to traditional normative and epistemic concerns of philosophy of science as much as it departs from those concerns—or, better, discloses a whole new set of connections to those traditional normative and epistemic concerns, ethical connections. If it is time philosophers of science integrate the ethical into our conception of scientific rationality, exploring how to make the ethics codes in the sciences adequate is an excellent place to start.

There are other reasons to suppose philosophers of science could play a significant role in the formulation of adequate ethics codes for the various sciences. Philosophers of science typically have a deep familiarity with one or more sciences and a sensitivity to issues that arise in connection with many sciences. At the same time, philosophers of science are typically not practitioners of any science and hence may be freer to move beyond the accustomed thought patterns of those who are. In addition, philosophers of science tend to have more time than others—especially scientists—to give to the kinds of issues relevant to ethics codes, since insights regarding such issues count more heavily in their professional lives and are considered more extraneous in scientists' professional lives. Most important, however, philosophers of science have already played significant roles in the formulation of ethics codes for the sciences. Feminist philosopher of science and philosopher of archaeology Alison Wylie, for example, chaired (with archaeologist Mark Lynott) the committee that drafted the 1996 Principles of Archaeological Ethics of the Society for American Archaeology, a code that was then adopted by other archaeological societies (such as the New Zealand Archaeological Association; see Society for American Archaeology 1996 and New Zealand Archaeological Association 1999). What made Wylie's contribution especially significant was that it involved forging a new disciplinary identity for archaeology, replete with new social/epistemic goals and responsibilities, in order to meet the entangled ethical/epistemic challenges now facing the field (see Wylie 1996, 1999, and 2005). Kristin Shrader-Frechette, another philosopher of science, has also made important contributions to the sciences' ethics codes. She has done extensive research on a wide variety of ethics codes, supported by the National Science Foundation and other sources, and has published some of her conclusions and recommendations in her book *Ethics of Scientific Research* (1994). Whether or not other philosophers of science have made similar contributions, Wylie and Shrader-Frechette document the important contributions philosophers of science could make to the formulation of adequate ethics codes.

PHILOSOPHY OF SCIENCE: A SUBJECT WITH A GREAT FUTURE

Nearly four decades ago, Paul Feyerabend wrote an essay entitled "Philosophy of Science: A Subject with a Great Past," in which he bemoaned the uselessness of the then-fashionable logical empiricism and went on to urge philosophers of science to pursue a very different kind of philosophy, one not only relevant to science but also fearless to criticize and even transform that science rather than conform to it. For this purpose, Feyerabend suggested that philosophers engage in a detailed study of primary sources in the history of science, at least those primary sources in which philosophy was closely involved with the science that was done and helped to shape its development. "It is to be hoped that such a concrete study will return to [philosophy of science] the excitement and usefulness it once possessed" (Feyerabend 1970, 183). Now, decades later, there is a need once again to bemoan the uselessness of philosophy of science and urge philosophers of science to criticize and even transform science rather than conform to it. This time, however, the need is to be met by ethical study, not historical—by broadening our conception of scientific rationality to encompass the ethical aspects of science, by acknowledging the inextricable interconnections of the ethical and the epistemic. It is to be hoped that by broadening our conception of scientific rationality in this way, we will indeed be able to return to philosophy of science the excitement and usefulness it once possessed—if not at the time of Feyerabend's Galileo, then at least at the time of the Vienna Circle's Neurath and Frank.

But exactly what is in the offing if we do broaden our conception of scientific rationality in this way? The kind of historical study applauded by Feyerabend—and Kuhn and Lakatos and Hanson and Toulmin and others—opened up new areas of inquiry for philosophers of science (such as scientific change) while it transformed other areas (such as scientific assessment). Will anything comparable happen if we now make efforts to interrelate the ethical and epistemic aspects of science? Certainly, scientific assessment, as we saw in chapter 3, will be transformed, and so will scientific development / scientific progress, if we now take into account the social values in science and the way they affect the wider society. And certainly, the various sciences' ethics codes will be a new area of inquiry. But there will be other new areas as well—such as scientists' research problems. Most philosophers of science today spend next to no time at all evaluating the research problems scientists work on or the applications of their results. What seems to be of interest is only what lies in between, the actual answers scientists come up with and their epistemic credentials. But defining appropriate research problems given real-world conditions— that is, with the relevant applications in mind—is absolutely crucial, ethically and epistemically. Consider two examples now very much in the news: AIDS research and cancer research.

First, AIDS research (see, for what follows, Hvistendahl 2006; Keefer 2006; Wainberg 2006; Wanjiku 2006; Wheeler 2006; UNAIDS 2006, 2008). Defined as a concern with the biomedical problem of how to deal with the AIDS virus, AIDS research has been a spectacular success. The AIDS antiretroviral drugs now available dramatically slow the course of the disease, and major efforts continue to be made toward developing an AIDS vaccine. Defined as a concern with the public-health problem of how to deal with those suffering from HIV/AIDS, however, AIDS research has been an abysmal failure. Indeed, worldwide only about 10% of HIV/AIDS sufferers currently take the expensive antiretroviral drugs—because of the lack of (public or private) funding to pay for them, or because of shortages of the drugs themselves, or because of the long journeys sometimes required to get to the health centers distributing the drugs, or because of the political or military problems sometimes associated with the travel (e.g., for Palestinians, who must go to hospitals in Israel to get the drugs), or because of governmental mishandling of the HIV/AIDS epidemic (as in China, whose government only recently acknowledged its AIDS problem), or because of the strong stigma still associated with the disease, or the ignorance and misinformation still surrounding it (e.g., among sex workers, who frequently do not understand the dangers of HIV/AIDS)—for these and other reasons only about 10% of HIV/AIDS sufferers currently take the antiretroviral drugs. As a result, more than 25 million people worldwide have already died from HIV/AIDS. In addition, another 33 million people now have contracted the disease. But 9 out of 10 of the people who have HIV do not know they have it (by 2006 only 12% of those who wanted to be tested were able to do so), and still other factors in addition to some of the ones mentioned above continue to encourage the spread of the disease—for example, the lack of access to condoms or the embarrassment about obtaining or using them or the lack of willingness on the part of men to use them or the lack of power on the part of women and girls to ensure their use. So, although the number of people on AIDS antiretroviral drugs has risen during the last few years, "the epidemic is outpacing the rate at which these drugs are being delivered. In 2007, the estimated number of new HIV infections was 2.5 times higher than the increase in the number of people on antiretroviral drugs in that year, underscoring the need for substantially greater success in preventing new HIV infections" (UNAIDS 2008, 15).

But none of this was researched and addressed until quite recently. Indeed, although it was 1981 when cases of AIDS first appeared, 1983 when France's Pasteur Institute and the U.S. National Institutes of Health isolated a pathogenic retrovirus from the cells of AIDS patients, and 1987 when the first AIDS therapy, AZT, was approved for use in the United States, it was only in the mid-1990s, according to AIDS researcher Mark Wainberg, director of the McGill University AIDS Centre, that "it was becoming apparent to many of us that unless something changed, only those in wealthy countries were going to have access to these therapies." And it was only 2000 when Wainberg, then president of the International AIDS Society, managed to "move the International AIDS Conference to Durban, South Africa, . . . so that the world's scientists and activists would experience the intensity and gravity of what pandemic AIDS had wrought on that region. . . . A quarter-century into the era of the AIDS epidemic, the global culture is finally starting to grapple with the disease as a nefarious and complex social and scientific problem" (Wainberg 2006, 57). Had the AIDS research problem been defined less narrowly 25 years earlier, as not only a biomedical problem but also a socioeconomic, cultural, and globalization problem, more relevant research with a better social outcome would have ensued.

Compare the situation with U.S. cancer research (see, for what follows, Proctor 1995; Epstein 1998; Leaf 2004; American Cancer Society 2008a, 2008b, and 2008c). Since the "war on cancer" was declared by the Nixon administration back in 1971, more than $200 billion has been spent in the United States on cancer research. Nevertheless, despite substantial progress on some fronts (e.g., childhood cancers), the percentage of Americans dying from cancer today is about what it was back in 1971— even correcting for the greater number of elderly today (those in whom cancer is most prevalent). And the percentage of Americans surviving for five years or more after a diagnosis of cancer has only increased from 50% to 63%. At the same time, the incidence of cancer has escalated to epidemic proportions: one in every two American men and one in every three American women will now get cancer sometime during their lifetime. Indeed, cancer is likely to become the leading cause of death in the United States within the next decade, replacing heart disease. The war on cancer, in short, is being lost—or, at least, it is not being won. And a big part of the failure surely relates to the way the war has been defined.

> The majority of funds distributed by cancer research bodies has gone either to efforts to improve treatment (especially surgery, radiation, and chemotherapy) or to efforts to understand the biological mechanisms involved in carcinogenesis. The emphasis, in other words, has been on the pragmatics of cures and the theoretical aspects of biochemical mechanisms, rather than on research into what causes cancer and (most important) what might be done to prevent it. (Proctor 1995, 265)

And this emphasis has produced few successes.

Regarding the efforts to improve treatment, for example, grants from the National Cancer Institute and other cancer-research bodies have frequently gone to study "preclinical models"—human cancer cells growing in immunocompromised mice or drosophila or nematodes that are then exposed to drugs that might be useful in treating people. But, reports Robert Weinberg, professor of biology at MIT and winner of the National Medal of Science for his discovery of both the first human oncogene and the first tumor-suppressor gene, "it's been well known for more than a decade, maybe two decades, that many of these preclinical human cancer models have very little predictive power in terms of how actual human beings—actual human tumors inside patients—will respond" (quoted in Leaf 2004, 84). Adds Eli Lilly research fellow Homer Pearce: "If you look at the millions and millions and millions of mice that have been cured, and you compare that to the relative success, or lack thereof, that we've achieved in the treatment of metastatic disease clinically, you realize that there just has to be something wrong with those models" (quoted in Leaf 2004, 84). Nonetheless, the use of such models is extremely widespread in both industry and academia (according to a 2004 search of the National Cancer Institute's online database, the cancer research community has published 150,855 experimental studies using mouse models alone), and the FDA continues to recognize these models as the gold standard for predicting the utility of drugs for clinical trials.

The efforts to understand the biological mechanisms involved in carcinogenesis have not fared much better. "The incentives are not aligned with the goals," explains Leonard Zwelling, vice president for research administration at M. D. Anderson, one of the major cancer-research centers in the United States. "If the goal is to cure cancer, you don't incentivize people to have little publications" (quoted in Leaf 2004, 82). But grants chiefly go to the researchers who focus on the very narrow—the very "little"—topics, that is, the very specific genetic or molecular mechanisms within the cancer cell or other tissue, not the broader, tougher, less researched topics more important to cancer survival such as metastasis(it is metastasis, after all, not localized cancer growth, that kills people with cancer 90% of the time), an organism-wide phenomenon that may involve dozens of processes but thereby poses problems of replicability. Nor is it clear that all of the emphasis on academic "basic research" understanding and publication is necessary. As Harvard pediatric pathologist Sidney Farber said (in congressional hearings in 1971) right at the very beginning of the war on cancer:

> We cannot wait for full understanding; the 325,000 patients with cancer who are going to die this year cannot wait; nor is it necessary, in order to make great progress in the cure of cancer, for us to have the full solution of all the problems of basic research. The history of medicine is replete with examples of cures obtained years, decades, and even centuries before the mechanism of action was understood for these cures—from vaccination, to digitalis, to aspirin. (quoted in Leaf 2004, 80)

Meanwhile, research into what causes cancer and what might be done to prevent it languishes. "There is substantial and long-standing evidence relating this epidemic to involuntary and avoidable exposures to industrial carcinogens in air, water, the workplace, and consumer products" (Epstein 1998, 511), carcinogens that require comprehensive research and out-reach prevention programs, including changes in the logic of industrial and business practices, to combat. There is also substantial and long-standing evidence that lifestyle choices both bear on cancer risk and are malleable. For example, an estimated 40% of the reduction in male cancer deaths between 1991 and 2003 has been attributed to smoking declines in the last half-century. But lifestyle choices, too, require comprehensive research and outreach programs to change—for example, research into why young people take up smoking in the first place and how they can be encouraged to quit (when we consider that the tobacco industry continues to out-spend states' tobacco-control programs by a ratio of nearly 24 to 1, we begin to appreciate the challenges posed by this area of research).

So, once again, an inappropriately defined research problem is directly implicated in the failure to achieve the goals of research. This, then, is a second new area of inquiry, besides the various sciences' ethics codes, that the broadening of philosophers' conception of scientific rationality will open up for philosophers of science: to articulate and even improve upon (i.e., suggest ethical/epistemic improvements to) the research problems scientists pursue in light of the goals scientists are trying (or should be trying) to accomplish. And this second new area of inquiry, in turn, sug-gests a third: to investigate the factors that affect the research problems scientists pursue in order ultimately to help bring about the (ethical/epistemic) improvement of those research problems. Regarding the cancer case discussed above, for example, "why is the bulk of cancer research dedicated to the improvement of treatment, when the more sensible approach would be to encourage prevention?" (Proctor 1995, 265). At least two answers have been offered. One deals with the culture of science:

> The sad truth is that cancer prevention is low prestige. Prevention is impover-ished in an age of heroic medicine, where the reward structure is heavily biased in favor of last-ditch, quick-burst, high-tech interventions and high-profile, Nobel Prize-potential basic science. In the field of research, this means exorbi-tant funding for therapies and molecular genetics and a more penurious approach to epidemiology, nutrition, health education, occupational health and safety, and behavioral and social science research—none of which will ever generate a Nobel Prize. (Proctor 1995, 267–268)

The second answer deals with economics: that the U.S. "cancer establishment"—the American Cancer Society and the National Cancer Institute—as well as major research institutions such as Memorial Sloan-Kettering have deep ties with the industries that both profit from the emphasis on treatment and basic research and would suffer if the emphasis turned to prevention and thence the regulation of the industrial carcinogens that help to cause the cancer in the first place. Indeed, Samuel Epstein, internationally recognized authority on the toxic and carcinogenic effects of environmental pollutants, has documented pervasive conflicts of interest in cancer-establishment employment and funding practices with the petrochemical, oil, media, mammography, and other industries and especially with the pharmaceutical (cancer drug) industry; according to Samuel Broder, former National Cancer Institute director, "The NCI has become what amounts to a government pharmaceutical company" (quoted in Epstein 1998, 496). As a result, "the priorities of the cancer establishment, the NCI and ACS, remain narrowly fixated on damage control—diagnosis and treatment—and on basic molecular research, with relative indifference to, if not always benign neglect of, prevention. . . . In short, the NCI and ACS bear major responsibility for losing the winnable war against cancer" (Epstein 1998, 511).

Of course, pursuing these kinds of answers will lead philosophers of science to still further new areas of inquiry—to the interconnected ethical/epistemic issues that now go by the name of the "commercialization of science" and the "politicization of science"; to the ethical/epistemic issues posed by the reward structure of science, not only the ways that structure sometimes motivates research on less important problems and blocks research on more important problems but also the ways it sometimes encourages scientific fraud and other sorts of scientific misconduct; to the related ethical/epistemic problems posed by the peer review system; and so on. Indeed, once we philosophers of science broaden our conception of scientific rationality to encompass the ethical aspects of science, the possibilities for useful, even transformative, science-relevant, and even science-policy-relevant research become endless.

FINAL THOUGHTS

There is a lot of commotion these days about public intellectuals—a lot of books and articles and discussions and debates about public intellectuals, a lot of lists of public intellectuals and rankings of public intellectuals. There are claims that public intellectuals have vanished into academia alongside claims that they are very much in the public eye thanks to the Internet, claims that they and their utopian ideas have become increasingly irrelevant in the fashionably postmodern academic scene alongside claims that they have become an increasingly important antidote in our highly commercialized academic scene, claims that they and their leftist ideas are "wrecking the university" alongside claims that the university and its professionalization are "wrecking" them. There are even disagreements about just what public intellectuals are and just what they do or should do. Thus, public intellectuals are said to be critical intellectuals who challenge and transform the status quo, but they are also said to be expert intellectuals who represent and legitimize it. Public intellectuals are said to be detached intellectuals, guardians of truth, committed to universal ideas and universal values, but they are also said to be engaged intellectuals, activists who articulate the interests and direct the aspirations of the social group to which they belong. And public intellectuals are said to be total intellectuals who might properly speak on any issue of current concern, but they are also said to be specific intellectuals who can properly deal only with specific public issues (see, e.g., Jacoby 1987; Kramer 1996; Posner 2001; Etzioni and Bowditch 2006; Misztal 2007). What is most striking to a philosopher of science, however, are the subjects of these claims, the public intellectuals themselves. For example, perusing the 2005 and 2008 lists of "Top 100 Public Intellectuals" from all over the world, selected by two journals (*Foreign Policy* in the United States and *Prospect* in the United Kingdom) and then ranked by polls of thousands of people (more than 20,000 people in 2005), we find a diversity of scientists, both natural and social, along with journalists and historians and feminist theorists and architects and businesspeople and statesmen and legal scholars and novelists and playwrights and social activists and religious leaders and art critics and here and there even philosophers—medieval and classical philosophers, ethicists and social and political philosophers, even a philosopher of mind (see *Prospect/Foreign Policy* 2005; *Foreign Policy/Prospect* 2008; see also Posner 2001). But philosophers of science are nowhere to be seen. Well, so what? We find no metaphysicians or epistemologists, either, though it is their endeavors—at least according to the editors and reviewers of some of our most prestigious U.S. philosophy journals—that today represent the very pinnacle of philosophical achievement. Still, the situation is unsettling. After all, science profoundly affects our society. But unlike most metaphysicians and epistemologists, we philosophers of science critically engage with science. So why does that engagement not put us into closer critical contact with society? Why do our philosophical endeavors, just like those of metaphysicians and epistemologists, still produce no public intellectuals?

Perhaps the question is ill conceived. Indeed, asking *why* philosophy of science produces no public intellectuals presupposes that philosophy of science *produces* no public intellectuals, at least at present. However, perhaps there are public intellectuals among philosophers of science today, public intellectuals who have somehow escaped the notice of the extant books and articles and lists and rankings regarding public intellectuals. But this simply will not do: to be a public intellectual just is not to escape such public notice. Well, then, perhaps there is a different reason for thinking our question ill conceived. After all, asking why philosophy of science produces no public intellectuals seems to suggest that philosophy of science *should* be producing public intellectuals, or at least that that is the kind of practitioners philosophy of science might plausibly produce. But perhaps a career as a public intellectual is just not suitable for a philosopher of science. Indeed, doing what it takes to be a public intellectual might be too "popular" or "journalistic" an activity or an activity too lacking in "legitimate authority" for a practitioner of an academic discipline like philosophy of science, and the threat of such epithets might properly deter philosophers of science from doing what it takes. But why is doing what it takes to be a public intellectual apparently *not* too popular or journalistic an activity or an activity too lacking in legitimate authority for practitioners of other academic fields such as biology or physics or history or economics or other professional fields such as the law or medicine or architecture or business, and why are the practitioners of these other fields not similarly deterred by such epithets? Indeed, given philosophy's historic penchant for "examining life," Socratic-style, and philosophy's historic track record for producing public intellectuals, philosophy would seem to be a prime source for public intellectuals in at least most of its areas of inquiry. So why not in philosophy of science?

But this suggests yet another reason for thinking our question ill conceived. Asking why philosophy of science produces no public intellectuals seems to suggest that philosophers of science *could be* public intellectuals— that we have what it takes. But public intellectuals are not only immensely distinguished intellectuals but also immensely influential intellectuals, influential not only in their own fields of specialization but in other fields as well and in the culture at large. They deal with the topics that people really care about, and just as often, they persuade people to really care about the topics with which they deal. What's more, they help to shape people's thoughts about those topics. They deal, in short, with the "important" topics, and they are the "important" thinkers on those topics, and they are exceedingly rare. So, as distinguished as some of today's philosophers of science are, perhaps they are simply not in the same league as these exceedingly rare individuals. But can it really be the case that *no* philosophers of science are as smart or as creative or as hardworking or as knowledgeable as the literary critics and psychologists and legal scholars and the rest who are public intellectuals today or that *all* philosophers of science lack these individuals' superior training and professional opportunities? More likely, philosophers of science just do not *do* what it takes.

But changes are on the horizon. For one, there seems to be a growing interest among philosophers of science in a more socially engaged and perhaps even a more politically engaged kind of philosophy of science. Indeed, panels on how to do more socially relevant philosophy of science are springing up at Philosophy of Science Association (PSA) meetings, and there has even been an American Philosophical Association mini-conference on the topic. What's more, PSA panels with titles such as "Race and Science" (2004), "Author Meets Critics: George Reisch's *How the Cold War Transformed Philosophy of Science*" (2006), and "Evidence, Uncertainty, and Risk: Challenges of Climate Science" (2008) are also springing up, and a new organization, Society for Philosophy of Science in Practice, has appeared. Added to this are conferences in both Europe and North America on science and values, the politicization of science, and the commercialization of science. True, all of this represents only a tiny proportion of what is currently going on in philosophy of science, but it is still a far larger tiny proportion than has been the case in many years. And there are now funding opportunities to support it. For example, the European Science Foundation is a sponsor of some of the recent and upcoming conferences on the politicization and the commercialization of science. And the U.S. National Science Foundation is now offering grants through its Science, Technology, and Society program for research projects dealing with such topic areas as ethics and values in science and technology, the impact of science and technology on the environment, and the interactions of science, technology, and society.

There are other changes as well—new concerns, for example, that philosophers of science will be hard pressed to ignore. Among the most prominent are the concerns surrounding the powerful new technologies now emerging, such as nanotechnology, genetic engineering, geoengineering, and robotics (see, e.g., Joy 2000; Roco and Bainbridge 2001; Schummer and Baird 2006; UNESCO 2006; Dean 2008). Take nanotechnology. Granted high-priority funding status in the United States in 2001 in view of its potential importance in a wide variety of areas, nanotechnology research has already garnered billions of dollars through the National Nanotechnology Initiative, and levels of funding in countries such as Japan and Germany are not far behind. Nevertheless, nanotechnology poses irreversible dangers as well as benefits—to human health (because of their small size, many nanomaterials are readily absorbed by the body and might cause highly toxic effects over time) and to the environment (producing a wholly new class of pollutants with new and unusual properties). Nanotechnology poses social dangers as well; the memory and other types of cognitive enhancements, diagnostic tools, and medical therapies it is due to deliver with the aid of taxpayer dollars will help propel the already privileged to new heights of privilege, exacerbating social inequalities. Still, the scientists and engineers who work in the area of nanotechnology as well as the other high-paced new technological areas often have neither the time nor the training to confront such concerns and often feel no need, given their perception of their work as purely factual and value-free. Philosophers of science might thus be in a position to help.

Finally, there now seems to be widespread acceptance (grudging or otherwise) of feminist philosophy of science, and feminist science-studies scholarship in general, among philosophers of science. This feminist scholarship, however, strives to be not only socially relevant but also socially transformative—strives to provide, in fact, "better knowledge and a better world, together" (Rouse 1997, 210). Its acceptance among philosophers of science—to the degree that it is accepted—thus signals the advent of a different kind of philosophy of science, a more activist kind of philosophy of science, which can be pursued in the service of any number of worthy causes in addition to feminist ones. At least, that has been the message and the hope of this book. Of course, pursuing such work will not guarantee that philosophers of science will ever become public intellectuals. But it could serve as a start.

References

Abplanalp, Judith M. 1983. "Premenstrual Syndrome: A Selective Review." *Women and Health* 8: 107–123.

Agin, Dan P. 2006. *Junk Science: How Politicians, Corporations, and Other Hucksters Betray Us*. New York: St. Martin's Press.

American Cancer Society. 2008a. *Cancer Facts and Figures 2008*. At http://www. cancer.org/downloads/STT/2008CAFFfinalsecured.pdf (accessed August 16, 2008).

———. 2008b. *Cancer Prevention & Early Detection Facts and Figures*. At http:// www.cancer.org/downloads/STT/CPED_2008.pdf (accessed August 6, 2008).

———. 2008c. *Cancer Statistics 2008: A Presentation from the American Cancer Society*. At http://www.cancer.org/docroot/PRO/content/PRO_1_1_Cancer_ Statistics_2008_Presentation.asp (accessed August 6, 2008).

American Chemical Society. 1994. "The Chemist's Code of Conduct." At http://www. chemistry.org/portal/a/c/s/1/acsdisplay.html?DOC=membership%5Cconduct. html (accessed September 19, 2006).

American Institute of Biological Sciences. 2002. "Ethics Statement." At http:// www.aibs.org/about-aibs/ethics_statement.html (accessed June 5, 2008).

American Physical Society. 2002. "Guidelines for Professional Conduct." At http:// www.aps.org/statements/02_2.cfm (accessed September 19, 2006).

American Psychological Association. 2002. "Ethical Principles of Psychologists and Code of Conduct." At http://www.apa.org/ethics (accessed September 18, 2006).

American Society for Biochemistry and Molecular Biology. 1998. "Code of Ethics." At http://www.asbmb.org/asbmb/site.nsf/Sub/CodeofEthics?opendocument (accessed October 18, 2006).

American Society for Microbiology. 2005. "Code of Ethics." At http://www.asm. org/ (accessed June 5, 2008).

Anastas, Paul T., and John C. Warner. 1998. *Green Chemistry: Theory and Practice*. Oxford: Oxford University Press.

Anderson, Elizabeth. 1995. "Knowledge, Human Interests, and Objectivity in Feminist Epistemology." *Philosophical Topics* 23, no. 2: 27–58.

———. 2004. "Uses of Value Judgments in Science: A General Argument, with Lessons from a Case Study of Feminist Research on Divorce." *Hypatia* 19, no. 1: 1–24.

Antony, Louise. 1993. "Quine as Feminist: The Radical Import of Naturalized Epistemology." In Louise Antony and Charlotte Witt, eds., *A Mind of One's Own: Feminist Essays on Reason and Objectivity*. Boulder, Colo.: Westview, 110–153.

———. 1995. "Sisters, Please, I'd Rather Do It Myself: A Defense of Individualism in Feminist Epistemology." *Philosophical Topics* 23, no. 2: 59–94.

Associazione Lucacoscioni. 2005. "Presentation World Congress." At http://www. lucacoscioni.it/node/6394 (accessed February 26, 2008).

Barnes, Barry, and R. G. A. Dolby. 1970. "The Scientific Ethos: A Deviant Viewpoint." *European Journal of Sociology* 11: 3–25.

Baty, Phil. 2005. "When Access to Data Is a Real Bone of Contention." *Times Higher Education Supplement* (November 25). At http://www.timeshighereducation. co.uk/story.asp?sectioncode=26&storycode=199922.

Baxter, Jane Eva. 2005. *The Archaeology of Childhood: Children, Gender, and Material Culture.* Walnut Creek, Calif.: AltaMira.

Bell, Robert. 1992. *Impure Science: Fraud, Compromise, and Political Influence in Scientific Research.* New York: Wiley.

Bergmann, Gustav. [1938] 1993. "Memories of the Vienna Circle: Letter to Otto Neurath (1938)." In Friedrich Stadler, ed., *Scientific Philosophy: Origins and Developments.* Dordrecht: Kluwer, 193–208.

Bernal, John Desmond. 1971. *Science in History,* Vol. 2: *The Scientific and Industrial Revolutions.* Cambridge, Mass.: MIT Press.

Biagioli, Mario. 1993. *Galileo, Courtier: The Practice of Science in the Culture of Absolutism.* Chicago and London: University of Chicago Press.

Biology and Gender Study Group. 1988. "The Importance of Feminist Critique for Contemporary Cell Biology." *Hypatia* 3: 61–76.

Blackwell, Richard J. 2006. *Behind the Scenes at Galileo's Trial.* Notre Dame, Ind.: University of Notre Dame Press.

Bleier, Ruth. 1984. *Sex and Gender.* New York: Pergamon.

Broad, William, and Nicholas Wade. 1982. *Betrayers of the Truth: Fraud and Deceit in the Halls of Science.* New York: Simon & Schuster.

Brumfiel, Geoff. 2002. "Misconduct Finding at Bell Labs Shakes Physics Community." *Nature* 419 (October 3): 419–421.

Bullock, Merry, and Sangeeta Panicker. 2003. "Ethics for All: Differences across Scientific Society Codes." *Science and Engineering Ethics* 9, no. 2: 159–170.

Bush, Vannevar. 1945. *Science: The Endless Frontier.* Washington, D.C.: U.S. Government Printing Office.

Campbell, Richmond. 1998. *Illusions of Paradox: A Feminist Epistemology Naturalized.* Oxford: Rowman and Littlefield.

———. 2001. "The Bias Paradox in Feminist Epistemology." In Nancy Tuana and Sandra Morgen, eds., *Engendering Rationalities.* Albany: State University of New York Press.

Caplan, Jeremy B., and Paula J. Caplan. 2005. "The Perseverative Search for Sex Differences in Mathematics Ability." In Ann M. Gallagher and James C. Kaufman, eds., *Gender Differences in Mathematics: An Integrative Psychological Approach.* Cambridge: Cambridge University Press, 25–47.

Carnap, Rudolf. 1963. "Intellectual Autobiography." In Paul Arthur Schilpp, ed., *The Philosophy of Rudolf Carnap.* La Salle, Ill.: Open Court, 1–84.

Carnap, Rudolf, Hans Hahn, and Otto Neurath. [1929] 1973. "The Scientific Conception of the World: The Vienna Circle." In Marie Neurath and Robert S. Cohen, eds., *Empiricism and Sociology.* Dordrecht: Reidel, 299–318. Originally published as *Wissenschaftliche Weltauffassung: Der Wiener Kreis* (Vienna: Artur Wolf, 1929). Also reprinted in Sahotra Sarkar, ed., *The Emergence of Logical Empiricism: From 1900 to the Vienna Circle* (New York and London: Garland, 1996), 321–340.

Cartwright, Nancy, Jordi Cat, Lola Fleck, and Thomas Uebel. 1996. *Otto Neurath: Philosophy between Science and Politics*. Cambridge: Cambridge University Press.

Ceci, Stephen J., and Wendy M. Williams, eds. 2007. *Why Aren't More Women in Science? Top Researchers Debate the Evidence*. Washington, D.C.: American Psychological Association.

———. 2010. *The Mathematics of Sex: How Biology and Society Conspire to Limit Talented Women and Girls*. New York: Oxford University Press.

Chrisler, John C., and Paula Caplan. 2002. "The Strange Case of Dr. Jekyll and Ms. Hyde: How PMS Became a Cultural Phenomenon and a Psychiatric Disorder." *Annual Review of Sex Research* 13: 274–306.

Committee on Equal Opportunities in Science and Engineering. 2007. *2005–2006 Biennial Report to Congress*. National Science Foundation. At http://www.nsf.gov/publications/pub_summ.jsp?ods_key=nsf07202 (accessed June 5, 2008).

Committee on Maximizing the Potential of Women in Academic Science and Engineering/Committee on Science, Engineering, and Public Policy, National Academy of Sciences, National Academy of Engineering, and Institute of Medicine. 2007. *Beyond Bias and Barriers: Fulfilling the Potential of Women in Academic Science and Engineering*. Washington, D.C.: The National Academies Press. At http://books.nap.edu/openbook/0309100429/gifmid/R1.gif (accessed June 5, 2008).

Conkey, Margaret W. 2008. "One Thing Leads to Another: Gendering Research in Archaeology." In Londa Schiebinger, ed., *Gendered Innovations in Science and Engineering*. Stanford: Stanford University Press, 43–64.

Conkey, Margaret W., and Sarah H. Williams. 1991. "Original Narratives: The Political Economy of Gender in Archaeology." In Micaela di Leonardo, ed., *Gender at the Crossroads of Knowledge: Feminist Anthropology in the Postmodern Era*. Berkeley and Los Angeles: University of California Press, 102–139.

Creager, Angela N., Elizabeth Lunbeck, and Londa Schiebinger, eds. 2001. *Feminism in Twentieth-Century Science, Technology, and Medicine*. Chicago: University of Chicago Press.

Dean, Cornelia. 2008. "Handle with Care." *New York Times* (August 12): D1, 4.

De Beauvoir, Simone. [1949] 1972. *The Second Sex*, trans. H. M. Pershley. New York: Penguin.

Deichmann, Ute. 1996. *Biologists under Hitler*, trans. Thomas Dunlap. Cambridge, Mass.: Harvard University Press.

Di Leonardo, Micaela, 1992. "Women, Culture, and Society Revisited: Feminist Anthropology for the 1990s." In Cheris Kramarae and Dale Spender, eds., *The Knowledge Explosion*. New York and London: Teachers College Press, 118–124.

Douglas, Heather. 2000. "Inductive Risk and Values in Science." *Philosophy of Science* 67, no. 4: 559–579.

Duhem, Pierre. [1908] 1969. *To Save the Phenomena: An Essay on the Idea of Physical Theory from Plato to Galileo*, trans. Edmund Doland and Chaninah Maschler. Chicago and London: University of Chicago Press.

Dupré, John. 2007. "Fact and Value." In John Dupré, Harold Kincaid, and Alison Wylie, eds., *Value-Free Science: Ideals and Illusions?* New York: Oxford University Press.

Easteal, Patricia Weiser. 1991. "Women and Crime: Premenstrual Issues." *Trends and Issues in Crime and Criminal Justice Series*, 31. At http://www.aic.gov.au/publications/tandi/tandi31.html (accessed February 10, 2007).

Eichler, Margrit. 1980. *The Double Standard: A Feminist Critique of Feminist Social Science*. New York: St. Martin's Press.

———. 1988. *Nonsexist Research Methods: A Practical Guide*. Boston: Allen & Unwin.

Elkana, Yehuda. 1982. "The Myth of Simplicity." In Gerald Holton and Yehuda Elkana, eds., *Albert Einstein: Historical and Cultural Perspectives*. Princeton, N.J.: Princeton University Press.

Epstein, Samuel S. 1998. *The Politics of Cancer Revisited*. Fremont Center, N.Y.: East Ridge.

Epstein, Steven. 1996. *Impure Science: AIDS, Activism, and the Politics of Knowledge*. Berkeley: University of California Press.

Estin, Ann Laquer. 2005. "Can Families Be Efficient? A Feminist Appraisal." In Martha Albertson Fineman and Terence Dougherty, eds., *Feminism Confronts Homo Economicus: Gender, Law, and Society*. Ithaca, N.Y.: Cornell University Press.

Etzioni, Amitai, and Alyssa Bowditch, eds. 2006. *Public Intellectuals: An Endangered Species?* Lanham, Md.: Rowman and Littlefield.

European Union. 2000. "Charter of Fundamental Rights of the European Union." *Official Journal of the European Communities*, 18.12.2000/C 364/1–22. At http://www.europarl.europa.eu/charter/pdf/text_en.pdf (accessed February 26, 2008).

———. n.d. "Frequently Asked Questions: Everything You Want to Know about the Charter." At http://ec.europa.eu/justice_home/unit/charte/en/faqs.html (accessed February 26, 2008).

Evers, Kathinka. 2001. *Standards for Ethics and Responsibility in Science: An Analysis and Evaluation of Their Content, Background and Function*. International Council for Science, Standing Committee on Responsibility and Ethics in Science. At http://www.icsu.org/Gestion/img/ICSU_DOC_DOWNLOAD/218_DD_FILE_Background_1.pdf (accessed May 31, 2008).

Fahrenkamp-Uppenbrink, Julia. 2002. "Chemistry Goes Green." *Science* 297, no. 5582 (August 2): 798.

Fausto-Sterling, Anne. 1985. *Myths of Gender*. New York: Basic Books.

———. 1992. *Myths of Gender*, 2nd ed. New York: Basic Books.

———. 2000. *Sexing the Body: Gender Politics and the Construction of Sexuality*. New York: Basic Books.

Fedigan, Linda Marie. 2001. "The Paradox of Feminist Primatology: The Goddess's Discipline?" In Angela N. Creager, Elizabeth Lunbeck, and Londa Schiebinger, eds., *Feminism in Twentieth-Century Science, Technology, and Medicine*. Chicago: University of Chicago Press, 46–72.

Fee, Elizabeth. 1983. "Women's Nature and Scientific Objectivity." In Marian Lowe and Ruth Hubbard, eds., *Women's Nature: Rationalizations of Inequality*. New York: Pergamon, 9–27.

Feldhay, Rivka. 1995. *Galileo and the Church: Political Inquisition or Critical Dialogue?* Cambridge and New York: Cambridge University Press.

Ferber, Marianne A., and Julie A. Nelson, eds. 1993. *Beyond Economic Man: Feminist Theory and Economics*. Chicago and London: University of Chicago Press.

———, eds. 2003. *Feminist Economics Today: Beyond Economic Man*. Chicago and London: University of Chicago Press.

Feyerabend, Paul. 1970. "Philosophy of Science: A Subject with a Great Past." In Roger H. Stuewer, ed., *Historical and Philosophical Perspectives of Science*. Minneapolis: University of Minnesota Press, 172–183.

Fineman, Martha Albertson, and Terence Dougherty, eds. 2005. *Feminism Confronts Homo Economicus: Gender, Law, and Society*. Ithaca, N.Y.: Cornell University Press.

Foreign Policy/Prospect. 2008. "Top 100 Public Intellectuals." At http://www.foreignpolicy.com/story/cms.php?story_id=4314&print=1 (accessed February 20, 2009).

Forman, Paul. 1987. "Behind Quantum Electronics: National Security as Basis for Physical Research in the United States, 1940–1960." *Historical Studies in the Physical and Biological Sciences* 18, no. 1: 149–229.

Frank, Philipp. 1949. *Modern Science and Its Philosophy*. Cambridge, Mass.: Harvard University Press.

———. 1951. *Relativity: A Richer Truth*. London: Jonathan Cape.

Geiger, Roger. 1994. "Review of *The Cold War and American Science: The Military-Industrial-Academic Complex at MIT and Stanford*." *Technology and Culture* 34: 629–631.

Gibbons, Michael, Camille Limoges, Helga Nowotny, Simon Schwartzman, Peter Scott, and Martin Trow. 1994. *The New Production of Knowledge: The Dynamics of Science and Research in Contemporary Societies*. London: Sage.

Giere, Ronald N. 1999. *Science without Laws*. Chicago: University of Chicago Press.

Gilman, Sander L. 1993. *Freud, Race, and Gender*. Princeton, N.J.: Princeton University Press.

Goodstein, David. 1995. "The Fading Myth of the Noble Scientist." In Nathaniel J. Pallone and James J. Hennessy, eds., *Fraud and Fallible Judgment: Varieties of Deception in the Social and Behavioral Sciences*. New Brunswick, N.J.: Transaction, 21–33.

Gordon, Jill. 1997. "John Stuart Mill and the 'Marketplace of Ideas.'" *Social Theory and Practice* 23, no. 2: 235–249.

Gough, Michael, ed. 2003. *Politicizing Science: The Alchemy of Policymaking*. Stanford, Calif.: Hoover Institution Press and George C. Marshall Institute.

Graham, Loren R. 1987. *Science, Philosophy, and Human Behavior in the Soviet Union*. New York: Columbia University Press.

Gura, Trisha. 1995. "Estrogen: Key Player in Heart Disease among Women." *Science* 269, no. 5225 (August 11): 771–773.

Guston, David H. 2000. *Between Politics and Science: Assuring the Integrity and Productivity of Research*. Cambridge: Cambridge University Press.

———. 2004. "Forget Politicizing Science. Let's Democratize Science!" *Issues in Science and Technology* (Fall): 25–28.

Halpern, Diane F. 2000. *Sex Differences in Cognitive Abilities*. Hillsdale, N.J.: Lawrence Erlbaum Associates.

Hamilton, Colin. 2008. *Cognition and Sex Differences*. New York: Palgrave Macmillan.

Hanson, Norwood Russell. 1958. *Patterns of Discovery: An Inquiry into the Conceptual Foundations of Science*. Cambridge: Cambridge University Press.

Harding, Sandra. 1991. *Whose Science? Whose Knowledge?* Ithaca, N.Y.: Cornell University Press.

Hegarty, Peter, and Carmen Buechel. 2006. "Androcentric Reporting of Gender Differences in APA Journals: 1965–2004." *Review of General Psychology* 10, no. 4: 377–389.

Heilbron, John L. 1987. "Applied History of Science." *Isis* 78: 552–563.

Heschel, Abraham J. (1965). *Who Is Man?* Stanford, Calif.: Stanford University Press.

Hess, David J. 1997. *Science Studies: An Advanced Introduction.* New York: New York University Press.

Hesse, Mary. 1980. *Revolutions and Reconstructions in the Philosophy of Science.* Brighton, U.K.: Harvester.

Hines, Melissa. 2001. "Book Review: Sex and Cognition." *Archives of Sexual Behavior* 30, no. 5: 551–554.

Hoag, Hannah. 2008. "The Greening of Chemistry." *Chemical Heritage* 26, no. 2 (Summer 2008): 26–30.

Horney, Karen. 1950. *The Collected Works of Karen Horney.* New York: W. W. Norton.

Horvath, Christopher. 2004. "The Developmental Challenge to Genetic Determinism: A Model Explanation for Sexual Attraction." Talk delivered at the Center for Philosophy of Science, University of Pittsburgh, February 13.

Hounshell, David A. 2001. "Epilogue: Rethinking the Cold War; Rethinking Science and Technology in the Cold War; Rethinking the Social Study of Science and Technology." *Social Studies of Science* 31, no. 2: 289–297.

Howard, Don. 2003. "Two Left Turns Make a Right: On the Curious Political Career of North-American Philosophy of Science at Mid-Century." In Alan Richardson and Gary Hardcastle, eds., *Logical Empiricism in North America.* Minneapolis: University of Minnesota Press.

Howson, Colin, ed. 1976. *Method and Appraisal in the Physical Sciences: The Critical Background to Modern Science, 1800–1905.* Cambridge: Cambridge University Press.

Hrdy, Sarah Blaffer. 1986. "Empathy, Polyandry, and the Myth of the Coy Female." In Ruth Bleier, ed., *Feminist Approaches to Science.* New York: Pergamon.

Hubbard, Ruth. 1979. "Have Only Men Evolved?" In Ruth Hubbard, Mary Sue Henifin, and Barbara Fried, eds., *Women Look at Biology Looking at Women: A Collection of Feminist Critiques.* Cambridge, Mass.: Schenkman.

Hvistendahl, Mara. 2006. "Advocacy: What's Changed—and What Hasn't, China." *Seed* 2, no. 6: 58.

Hyde, Janet Shibley. 2000. "Review: A Gendered Brain?" The Journal of Sex Research 37, no. 2: 191.

Interlandi, Jeneen. 2006. "An Unwelcome Discovery." *New York Times* (October 22). At http://www.nytimes.com/2006/10/22/magazine/22sciencefraud.html?_r=1&adxnnl=1&adxnnlx=1241878197-IgbuM0fy8QyFTgLAPLl5hg.

International Council for Science's Standing Committee on Responsibility and Ethics in Science. 1999. "Ethics and the Responsibility of Science: Background Paper," Forum I, Session 11 ("Introduction"). At http://www.unesco.org/science/wcs/background/ethics.htm (accessed September 17, 2006).

Iverson, Margot, Mark S. Frankel, and Sanyin Siang. 2003. "Scientific Societies and Research Integrity: What Are They Doing and How Well Are They Doing It?" *Science and Engineering Ethics* 9, no. 2: 141–158.

Jacoby, Russell. 1987. *The Last Intellectuals: American Culture in the Age of Academe.* New York: Basic Books.

Jensen, Allan Astrup. 2001. *Establishment of a European Green and Sustainable Chemistry Award.* Copenhagen: European Environment Agency.

Jewish Virtual Library. 2007. "Nazi Medical Experiments." At http://www.jewishvirtuallibrary.org/jsource/Holocaust/medtoc.html.

Johnson, George. 2002. "At Lawrence Berkeley, Physicists Say a Colleague Took Them for a Ride." *New York Times* (October 15): F1. At http://www.nytimes. com/2002/10/15/science/at-lawrence-berkeley-physicists-say-a-colleague-took-them-for-a-ride.html.

Joy, Bill. 2000. "Why the Future Doesn't Need Us." *Wired* 8, no. 4. At http://www. wired.com/wired/archive/8.04/joy_pr.html (accessed August 16, 2008).

Joyce, Rosemary. 2000. "Girling the Girl and Boying the Boy: The Production of Adulthood in Ancient Mesoamerica." *World Archaeology* 31, no. 3: 473–483.

Judson, Horace Freeland. 2004. *The Great Betrayal: Fraud in Science*. Orlando, Fla.: Harcourt.

Karafyllis, Nicole C., and Gotlind Ulshofer, eds. 2008. *Sexualized Brains: Scientific Modeling of Emotional Intelligence from a Cultural Perspective*. Cambridge, Mass.: MIT Press.

Katz, Jay. 1996. "The Nuremberg Code and the Nuremberg Trial: A Reappraisal." *Journal of the American Medical Association* 276, no. 20: 1662–1666.

Keefer, Michael. 2006. "The Vaccine: Report from the Lab, USA." *Seed* 2, no. 6: 66.

Keller, Evelyn Fox. 1983. *A Feeling for the Organism*. San Francisco: W. H. Freeman.

———. 1985. *Reflections on Gender and Science*. New Haven, Conn.: Yale University Press.

Kevles, Daniel. 1990. "Cold War and Hot Physics: Science, Security, and the American State, 1945–56." *Historical Studies in the Physical and Biological Sciences* 20, no. 2: 239–264.

———. 1998. *The Baltimore Case: A Trial of Politics, Science, and Character*. New York: W. W. Norton.

Kieper, Adam, Michael Gough, Steven Hayward, Robert Walker, and Wiliam O'Keefe. 2004. "Who Is Politicizing Science? Understanding the Interactions and Interests in Science and Politics." Washington Roundtable on Science and Public Policy. Washington, D.C.: George C. Marshall Institute. At http://www. marshall.org.

Kimura, Doreen. 2000a. "Don't Discriminate with Grants." *National Post* (January 8): B7. At http://www.sfu.ca/~dkimura/.

———. 2000b. *Sex and Cognition*. Cambridge, Mass.: MIT Press.

———. 2001. "Biological Constraints on Parity between the Sexes." *Psynopsis* 23 (Winter): 3. At http://www.sfu.ca/~dkimura/.

———. 2002a. "Preferential Hiring of Women." *UBC Reports* (January 10): 2.

———. 2002b. "Sex Hormones Influence Human Cognitive Pattern." *Neuroendocrinology Letters* 23 (suppl. 4): 67–77.

———. 2004a. "Human Sex Differences in Cognition: Fact, Not Predicament." *Sexualities, Evolution & Gender* 6: 45–53.

———. 2004b. "Hysteria Trumps Academic Freedom." *Vancouver Sun* (February 1): A13.

———. 2006. "'Underrepresentation' or Misrepresentation?" In Stephen J. Ceci and Wendy M. Williams, eds., *Why Aren't More Women in Science?* Washington, D.C.: American Psychological Association, 39–46.

Kitcher, Philip. 1993. *The Advancement of Science. Science without Legend, Objectivity without Illusion*. New York: Oxford University Press.

———. 2001. *Science, Truth, and Democracy*. New York: Oxford University Press.

Kitcher, Philip, and Nancy Cartwright. 1996. "Science and Ethics: Reclaiming Some Neglected Questions." *Perspectives on Science* 4, no. 2: 145–153.

Kline, Stephen J., and Nathan Rosenberg. 1986. "An Overview of Innovation." In Ralph Landau and Nathan Rosenberg, eds., *The Positive Sum Strategy: Harnessing Technology for Economic Growth*. Washington, D.C.: National Academy Press, 275–305.

Knorr-Cetina, Karin. 1981. *The Manufacture of Knowledge*. Oxford: Pergamon.

Knorr-Cetina, Karin, and Michael Mulkay, eds. 1983. *Science Observed: Perspectives on the Social Study of Science*. London: Sage.

Kourany, Janet A. 2000. "A Successor to the Realism/Antirealism Question." *Philosophy of Science* 67 (Proceedings): S87-S101.

Kramer, Lloyd. 1996. "Habermas, Foucault, and the Legacy of Enlightenment Intellectuals." In Leon Fink, Stephen T. Leonard, and Donald M. Reid, eds., *Intellectuals and Public Life: Between Radicalism and Reform*. Ithaca, N.Y., and London: Cornell University Press, 29–50.

Kuhn, Thomas S. 1962. *The Structure of Scientific Revolutions*. Chicago: University of Chicago Press.

———. 1963. "The Function of Dogma in Scientific Research." In A. C. Crombie, ed., *Scientific Change*. New York: Basic Books, 347–369.

———. 1970. "Postscript—1969." In Thomas S. Kuhn, *The Structure of Scientific Revolutions*, 2nd ed. Chicago: University of Chicago Press, 174–210.

———. 1977. "Objectivity, Value Judgment, and Theory Choice." In Thomas S. Kuhn, *The Essential Tension: Selected Studies in Scientific Tradition and Change*. Chicago: University of Chicago Press.

Ladner, Joyce. 1971. *Tomorrow's Tomorrow: The Black Woman*. Garden City, N.Y.: Doubleday.

LaFollette, Marcel. 1992. *Stealing into Print: Fraud, Plagiarism, and Misconduct in Scientific Publishing*. Berkeley: University of California Press.

Lakatos, Imre. 1970. "Falsification and the Methodology of Scientific Research Programmes." In Imre Lakatos and Alan Musgrave, eds., *Criticism and the Growth of Knowledge*. Cambridge: Cambridge University Press.

———. 1976. "History of Science and Its Rational Reconstructions." In C. Howson, ed., *Method and Appraisal in the Physical Sciences*. Cambridge: Cambridge University Press.

Lalli, Chiara, and Carmen Sorrentino, eds. 2007. *Proceedings of the World Congress for Freedom of Scientific Research*. Rome: Cooper-Darwin. At http://www.freedomofresearch.org/node/132 (accessed on February 26, 2008).

Langreth, Robert, and Matthew Herper. 2005. "Merck's Deleted Data." *Forbes* (December 8). At http://www.forbes.com/2005/12/08/merck-vioxx-lawsuits_cx_mh_1208vioxx.html.

Latour, Bruno. 1987. *Science in Action: How to Follow Scientists and Engineers through Society*. Cambridge, Mass.: Harvard University Press.

Latour, Bruno, and Steve Woolgar. 1979. *Laboratory Life: The Social Construction of Scientific Facts*. Beverly Hills, Calif.: Sage.

Laudan, Larry. 1977. *Progress and Its Problems*. Berkeley: University of California Press.

Leaf, Clifton. 2004. "Why We're Losing the War on Cancer (and How to Win It)." *Fortune* 77 (March 22): 77–92.

Leslie, Stuart W. 1993. *The Cold War and American Science: The Military-Industrial-Academic Complex at MIT and Stanford*. New York: Columbia University Press.

Lewontin, Richard C. 2004. "Dishonesty in Science." *New York Review of Books* 51, no. 18 (November 18). At http://www.nybooks.com/articles/17563.

Lewontin, Richard, and Richard Levins. 1976. "The Problem of Lysenkoism." In Hilary Rose and Steven Rose, eds., *The Radicalisation of Science: Ideology of/in the Natural Sciences*. London: Macmillan, 32–64.

Lock, Stephen, Frank Wells, and Michael Farthing, eds. 2001. *Fraud and Misconduct in Biomedical Research*, 3rd ed. London: British Medical Journal Books.

Long, J. Scott, Paul Allison, and Robert McGinness. 1979. "Entrance into the Academic Career." *American Sociological Review* 44: 816–830.

Longino, Helen. 1990. *Science as Social Knowledge: Values and Objectivity in Scientific Inquiry*. Princeton, N.J.: Princeton University Press.

———. 1994. "In Search of Feminist Epistemology," *Monist* 77: 472–485.

———. 1995. "Gender, Politics, and the Theoretical Virtues." *Synthese* 104: 383–397.

———. 1997. "Cognitive and Non-Cognitive Values in Science: Rethinking the Dichotomy." In Lynn Hankinson Nelson and Jack Nelson, eds., *Feminism, Science, and the Philosophy of Science*. Dordrecht, Neth.: Kluwer, 39–58.

———. 2002. *The Fate of Knowledge*. Princeton, N.J., and Oxford: Princeton University Press.

———. 2008. "Values, Heuristics, and the Politics of Knowledge." In Martin Carrier, Don Howard, and Janet Kourany, eds., *The Challenge of the Social and the Pressure of Practice: Science and Values Revisited*. Pittsburgh: University of Pittsburgh Press, 68–86.

Mann, Charles. 1995. "Women's Health Research Blossoms." *Science* 269, no. 5225 (August 11): 766–770.

Marburger, John H. III. 2004. *Statement of the Honorable John H. Marburger III on Scientific Integrity in the Bush Administration*. At http://www.ostp.gov/html/ucs/SummaryResponsetoCongressonUCSDocumentApril2004.pdf.

Marecek, Jeanne. 1995. "Psychology and Feminism: Can This Relationship Be Saved?" In Domna C. Stanton and Abigail J. Stewart, eds., *Feminisms in the Academy*. Ann Arbor, Mich.: University of Michigan Press, 101–132.

Martinson, Brian, Melissa Anderson, and Raymond De Vries. 2005. "Scientists Behaving Badly." *Nature* 435 (June 9): 737–738.

McCook, Alison. 2005. "Journal Prints Rejected Paper—As Ad." *The Scientist*. At http://www.biomedcentral.com/news/20050429/02.

McCumber, John. 2001. *Time in the Ditch: American Philosophy and the McCarthy Era*. Evanston, Ill.: Northwestern University Press.

McGarity, Thomas, and Wendy Wagner. 2008. *Bending Science: How Special Interests Corrupt Public Health Research*. Cambridge, Mass.: Harvard University Press.

McGinness, Robert, Paul Allison, and J. Scott Long. 1982. "Postdoctoral Training in Bioscience: Allocation and Outcomes." *Social Forces* 60: 701–722.

McMullin, Ernan. 1968. "What Do Physical Models Tell Us?" In B. van Rootselaar and J. F. Staal, eds., *Logic, Methodology, and Philosophy of Science III*. Amsterdam: North-Holland, 385–396.

———. 1976. "The Fertility of Theory and the Unit of Appraisal in Science." In R. S. Cohen, P.K. Feyerabend, and M.W. Wartofsky, eds., *Essays in Memory of Imre Lakatos*. Dordrecht: Reidel, 395–432.

———. 1983. "Values in Science." In Peter Asquith and Tom Nickles, eds., *PSA 1982*, vol. 2. East Lansing, Mich.: Philosophy of Science Association.

———. 1984. "The Rational and the Social in the History of Science." In James Brown, ed., *Scientific Rationality: The Sociological Turn*. Dordrecht: Reidel.

Meinert, Curtis L. 1995. "The Inclusion of Women in Clinical Trials." *Science* 269, no. 5225 (August 11): 795–796.

Merchant, Carolyn. 1980. *The Death of Nature: Women, Ecology, and the Scientific Revolution.* San Francisco: Harper & Row.

Merton, Robert K. [1938] 1973. "Science and the Social Order." In Norman W. Storer, ed., *The Sociology of Science: Theoretical and Empirical Investigations.* Chicago: University of Chicago Press, 254–266.

———. [1942] 1973. "The Normative Structure of Science." In Norman W. Storer, ed., *The Sociology of Science: Theoretical and Empirical Investigations.* Chicago: University of Chicago Press, 267–278.

———. [1957] 1973. "Priorities in Scientific Discovery." In Norman W. Storer, ed., *The Sociology of Science: Theoretical and Empirical Investigations.* Chicago: University of Chicago Press, 286–324.

Meskell, Lynn. 1998. "Intimate Archaeologies: The Case of Kha and Merit." *World Archaeology* 29, no. 3: 363–379.

Mill, John Stuart. [1859] 1956. *On Liberty*, ed. Currin V. Shields. Indianapolis: Bobbs-Merrill.

Misztal, Barbara A. 2007. *Intellectuals and the Public Good: Creativity and Civil Courage.* New York: Cambridge University Press.

Mitroff, Ian. 1974. "Norms and Counternorms in a Select Group of the Apollo Moon Scientists: A Case Study of the Ambivalence of Scientists. *American Sociological Review* 39: 579–595.

Mulkay, Michael J. 1976. "Norms and Ideology in Science." *Social Science Information* 15: 637–656.

———. 1980. "Interpretation and the Use of Rules: The Case of the Norms of Science." In T. F. Gieryn, ed., *Science and Social Structure: A Festschrift for Robert K. Merton.* New York: New York Academy of Sciences, 111–125.

Mutari, Ellen, Heather Boushey, and William Fraher IV. 1997. *Gender and Political Economy: Incorporating Diversity into Theory and Policy.* Armonk, N.Y.: M. E. Sharpe.

National Women's Law Center. 2009. "Congress Must Act to Close the Wage Gap for Women: Facts on Women's Wages and Pending Legislation" (April). At http://www.nwlc.org/pdf/PayEquityFactSheetFinal.pdf (accessed January 19, 2010).

Nelson, Donna J. 2007. *A National Analysis of Minorities in Science and Engineering Faculties at Research Universities.* Diversity in Science Association. At http://cheminfo.ou.edu/~djn/diversity/Faculty_Tables_FY07/07Report.pdf (accessed June 5, 2008).

Nelson, Julie A. 1996a. *Feminism, Objectivity and Economics.* London and New York: Routledge.

———. 1996b. "The Masculine Mindset of Economic Analysis." *Chronicle of Higher Education* 42, no. 42: B3.

Neurath, Otto. [1913] 1983. "The Lost Wanderers of Descartes and the Auxiliary Motive (On the Psychology of Decision)." In Robert S. Cohen and Marie Neurath, eds. and trans., *Otto Neurath, Philosophical Papers, 1913–1946.* Dordrecht: Reidel, 1–12.

———. [1928] 1973. "Personal Life and Class Struggle." In Marie Neurath and Robert S. Cohen, eds., *Empiricism and Sociology.* Dordrecht: Reidel, 249–298,

———. [1930] 1983. "Ways of the Scientific World-Conception." In Robert S. Cohen and Marie Neurath, eds. and trans., *Otto Neurath, Philosophical Papers, 1913–1946.* Dordrecht: Reidel, 32–47.

————. [1931] 1973. "Empirical Sociology." In Marie Neurath and Robert S. Cohen, eds., *Empiricism and Sociology*. Dordrecht: Reidel, 319–421.

————. [1934] 1983. "Radical Physicalism and the 'Real World.'" In Robert S. Cohen and Marie Neurath, eds. and trans., *Otto Neurath, Philosophical Papers, 1913–1946*. Dordrecht: Reidel, 100–114.

————. [1935] 1983. "The Unity of Science as a Task." In Robert S. Cohen and Marie Neurath, eds. and trans., *Otto Neurath, Philosophical Papers, 1913–1946*. Dordrecht: Reidel, 115–120.

————. 1938. "Unified Science as Encyclopedic Integration." In Otto Neurath, Rudolf Carnap, and Charles Morris, eds., *International Encyclopedia of Unified Science*, vol. 1. Chicago: University of Chicago Press, 1–27. Reprinted in Sahotra Sarkar, ed., *Science and Philosophy in the Twentieth Century: Basic Works of Logical Empiricism* (New York and London: Garland, 1996), 309–335.

Newton-Smith, William. 1981. *The Rationality of Science*. Oxford: Routledge and Kegan Paul.

New Zealand Archaeological Association. 1999. "NZAA Code of Ethics." At http://www.nzarchaeology.org/ethics.htm (accessed September 16, 2006).

Nickles, Thomas, ed. 1978. *Scientific Discovery: Case Studies*. Dordrecht: Reidel.

————, ed. 1980. *Scientific Discovery, Logic, and Rationality*. Boston: Kluwer.

Nowotny, Helga, Peter Scott, and Michael Gibbons. 2001. *Rethinking Science: Knowledge and the Public in an Age of Uncertainty*. Cambridge: Polity.

Okin, Susan. 1999. *Is Multiculturalism Bad for Women?* Princeton, N.J.: Princeton University Press.

Osler, Margaret J. 1998. "Mixing Metaphors: Science and Religion or Natural Philosophy and Theology in Early Modern Europe." *History of Science* 36: 91–113.

Parlee, Mary Brown. 1973. "The Premenstrual Syndrome." *Psychological Bulletin* 80: 454–465.

Pinker, Steven. 2002. *The Blank Slate: The Modern Denial of Human Nature*. New York: Viking Penguin.

————. 2005. "The Science of Gender and Science: Pinker vs. Spelke—A Debate." Harvard University Mind/Brain/Behavior Initiative, May 16. At http://www.edge.org/3rd_culture/debate05/debate05_index.html.

Polanyi, Michael. 1951. *The Logic of Liberty*. Chicago: University of Chicago Press.

————. 1962. "The Republic of Science: Its Political and Economic Theory." *Minerva* 1: 54–74.

————. 1967. *The Tacit Dimension*. New York: Anchor.

Posner, Richard A. 2001. *Public Intellectuals: A Study of Decline*. Cambridge, Mass.: Harvard University Press.

Price, Derek J. de Solla. 1965. "Is Technology Historically Independent of Science? A Study in Statistical Historiography." *Technology and Culture* 6, no. 4: 553–568.

Price, Don K. 1965. *The Scientific Estate*. Cambridge, Mass.: Harvard University Press.

Proctor, Robert N. 1988. *Racial Hygiene: Medicine under the Nazis*. Cambridge, Mass.: Harvard University Press.

————. 1991. *Value-Free Science? Purity and Power in Modern Knowledge*. Cambridge, Mass.: Harvard University Press.

———. 1995. *Cancer Wars: How Politics Shapes What We Know and Don't Know about Cancer*. New York: Basic Books.

———. 1999. *The Nazi War on Cancer*. Princeton, N.J.: Princeton University Press.

———. 2000. "Nazi Science and Nazi Medical Ethics: Some Myths and Misconceptions." *Perspectives in Biology and Medicine* 43, no. 3: 335–346.

Prospect/Foreign Policy. 2005. "Top 100 Public Intellectuals." At http://www. infoplease.com/spot/topintellectuals.html (accessed February 20, 2009).

Putnam, Hilary. 2002. *The Collapse of the Fact/Value Dichotomy*. Cambridge, Mass.: Harvard University Press.

Rabounski, Dmitri. 2006. "Declaration of Academic Freedom (Scientific Human Rights)." *Progress in Physics* 1 (January): 57–60. At http://www.geocities.com/ptep_online/rights.html.

Reichenbach, Hans. 1938. *Experience and Prediction*. Chicago: University of Chicago Press.

Reisch, George. 2005. *How the Cold War Transformed Philosophy of Science: To the Icy Slopes of Logic*. New York: Cambridge University Press.

Reskin, Barbara. 1976. "Sex Differences in Status Attainment in Science: The Case of Postdoctoral Fellowships." *American Sociological Review* 41: 597–613.

Rittenhouse, C. Amanda. 1991. "The Emergence of Premenstrual Syndrome as a Social Problem." *Social Problems* 38, no. 3: 412–425.

Roco, Mihail C., and William Sims Bainbridge. 2001. *Societal Implications of Nanoscience and Nanotechnology*. Dordrecht and Boston: Springer.

Roll-Hansen, Nils. 2005. *The Lysenko Effect: The Politics of Science*. New York: Humanity Books.

Rose, Steven. 2009. "Should Scientists Study Race and IQ? No: Science and Society Do Not Benefit." *Nature* 457 (7231): 786–788.

Rosenberg, Nathan. 1986. "The Impact of Technological Innovation: A Historical View." In Ralph Landau and Nathan Rosenberg, eds., *The Positive Sum Strategy: Harnessing Technology for Economic Growth*. Washington, D.C.: National Academy Press, 17–32.

Rosser Sue. 1990. *Female-Friendly Science: Applying Women's Studies Methods and Theories to Attract Students*. New York: Pergamon.

———. 1994. *Women's Health—Missing from U.S. Medicine*. Bloomington and Indianapolis: Indiana University Press.

Rouse, Joseph. 1997. "Feminism and the Social Construction of Scientific Knowledge." In Lynn Hankinson Nelson and Jack Nelson, eds., *Feminism, Science, and the Philosophy of Science*. Dordrecht: Kluwer.

Royal Society of Chemistry. 2006. "Announcing the 2005 Canadian Green Chemistry Medal." At http://www.rsc.org/publishing/journals/gc/news/green. asp (accessed July 10, 2008).

Ruse, Michael. 1999. *Mystery of Mysteries: Is Evolution a Social Construction?* Cambridge, Mass.: Harvard University Press.

Sanday, Peggy. 1981. "The Socio-cultural Context of Rape: A Cross-cultural Study." *Journal of Social Issues* 37, no. 4: 5–27.

———. 1990. *Fraternity Gang Rape: Sex, Brotherhood and Privilege on Campus*. New York: New York University Press.

———. 1996. *A Woman Scorned: Acquaintance Rape on Trial*. New York: Doubleday.

Santosuosso, Amedeo, Elisabetta Fabio, and Valentina Sellaroli. 2007. "What Constitutional Protection for Freedom of Scientific Research?" In Chiara Lalli and Carmen Sorrentino, eds., *Proceedings of the World Congress for Freedom of Scientific Research*. Rome: Cooper-Darwin, 275–283.

Sarewitz, Daniel. 2004. "How Science Makes Environmental Controversies Worse." *Environmental Science and Policy* 7: 385–403.

———. 2006. "Institutional Ecology and Societal Outcomes." NSF Workshop on the Social Organization of Science and Science Policy, July 13–14. At http://www.cspo.org/ourlibrary/papers/Sarewitz.pdf (accessed August 17, 2006).

Sarewitz, Daniel, Guillermo Foladori, Noela Invernizzi, and Michele S. Garfinkel. 2004. "Science Policy in Its Social Context." *Philosophy Today* suppl.: 67–83.

Schiebinger, Londa. 1989. *The Mind Has No Sex?* Cambridge, Mass.: Harvard University Press.

———. 1999. *Has Feminism Changed Science?* Cambridge, Mass.: Harvard University Press.

Schmidt, Robert, and Barbara Voss, eds. 2000. *Archaeologies of Sexuality*. London: Routledge.

Schummer, Joachim, and Davis Baird. 2006. *Nanotechnology Challenges: Implications for Philosophy, Ethics and Society*. Hackensack, N.J.: World Scientific.

Schweber, Silvan. 2000. *In the Shadow of the Bomb: Bethe, Oppenheimer, and the Moral Responsibility of the Scientist*. Princeton, N.J.: Princeton University Press.

Shapere, Dudley. 1974. "Scientific Theories and Their Domains." In Frederick Suppe, ed., *The Structure of Scientific Theories*. Urbana, Ill.: University of Illinois Press, 518–565.

———. 1984. *Reason and the Search for Knowledge*. Dordrecht: Reidel.

Shapin, Steven, and Simon Schaffer. 1985. *Leviathan and the Air-Pump: Hobbes, Boyle, and the Experimental Life*. Princeton, N.J.: Princeton University Press.

Sherif, Carolyn Wood. 1979. "Bias in Psychology." In Julia Sherman and Evelyn Torton Beck, eds., *The Prism of Sex: Essays in the Sociology of Knowledge*. Madison: University of Wisconsin Press.

Sherman, Linda Ann, Robert Temple, and Ruth B. Merkatz. 1995. "Women in Clinical Trials: An FDA Perspective." *Science* 269, no. 5225 (August 11): 793–795.

Shrader-Frechette, Kristin. 1994. *Ethics of Scientific Research*. Lanham, Md.: Rowman and Littlefield.

Society for American Archaeology. 1996. "Principles of Archaeological Ethics." At http://www.saa.org/public/resources/ethics.html (accessed August 16, 2008).

Solomon, Miriam. 2001. *Social Empiricism*. Cambridge, Mass.: MIT Press.

Solovey, Mark. 2001. "Project Camelot and the 1960s Epistemological Revolution: Rethinking the Politics-Patronage-Social Science Nexus." *Social Studies of Science* 31, no. 2: 171–206.

Stanley, Liz, and Sue Wise. 1983. *Breaking Out: Feminist Consciousness and Feminist Research*. London: Routledge & Kegan Paul.

Stefan, Susan. 1996. "Reforming the Provision of Mental Health Treatment." In Kary L. Moss, ed., *Man-made Medicine: Women's Health, Public Policy, and Reform*. Durham, N.C., and London: Duke University Press, 195–218.

Stokes, Donald E. 1997. *Pasteur's Quadrant: Basic Science and Technological Innovation*. Washington, D.C.: Brookings Institution Press.

Suppe, Frederick. 1974. "The Search for Philosophic Understanding of Scientific Theories." In Frederick Suppe, ed., *The Structure of Scientific Theories*. Urbana, Ill.: University of Illinois Press, 1–241.

Swazey, Judith P., Melissa S. Anderson, and Karen Seashore Louis. 1993. "Ethical Problems in Academic Research." *American Scientist* 81, no. 6: 542–553.

Toulmin, Stephen. 1953. *The Philosophy of Science: An Introduction*. London: Hutchinson & Co.

———. 1961. *Foresight and Understanding*. New York: Harper and Row.

Uebel, Thomas. 1998. "Enlightenment and the Vienna Circle's Scientific World-Conception." In Amelie Oksenberg Rorty, ed., *Philosophers on Education: Historical Perspectives*. London and New York: Routledge, 418–438.

———. 2003. "History of Philosophy of Science and the Politics of Race and Ethnic Exclusion." In Michael Heidelberger and Friedrich Stadler, eds., *Wissenschaftsphilosophie und Politik, Philosophy of Science and Politics*. Vienna: Springer-Verlag, 91–117.

UNAIDS. 2006. "2006 Report on the Global AIDS Epidemic: A UNAIDS 10th Anniversary Special Edition." At http://data.unaids.org/pub/GlobalReport/2006/2006_GR-ExecutiveSummary_en.pdf (accessed August 10, 2008).

———. 2008. "2008 Report on the Global AIDS Epidemic." At http://www.unaids.org:80/en/KnowledgeCentre/HIVData/GlobalReport/2008/ (accessed August 10, 2008).

UNESCO. 2006. *The Ethics and Politics of Nanotechnology*. Paris: UNESCO. At http://unesdoc.unesco.org/images/0014/001459/145951e.pdf (accessed August 20, 2008).

UNFPA (United Nations Population Fund). 2005. "Violence against Women Fact Sheet: State of World Population 2005." At http://www.unfpa.org/swp/2005/presskit/factsheets/facts_vaw.htm (accessed August 2008).

UNICEF (United Nations Children's Fund). 2006. *The State of the World's Children 2007: Women and Children—The Double Dividend of Gender Equality*. New York: UNICEF. At http://www.unicef.org/sowc07/docs/sowc07.pdf (accessed August 2008).

UNIFEM (United Nations Development Fund for Women). 2007. "Violence against Women—Facts and Figures." At http://www.unifem.org/attachments/gender_issues/violence_against_women/facts_figures_violence_against_women_2007.pdf (accessed August 2008).

Union of Concerned Scientists. 2004a. *Restoring Scientific Integrity in Policy Making*. At http://www.ucsusa.org/rsi.

———. 2004b. *Scientific Integrity in Policymaking: An Investigation into the Bush Administration's Misuse of Science*. At http://www.ucsusa.org/rsi.

———. 2004c. *Scientific Integrity in Policy Making: Further Investigation of the Bush Administration's Misuse of Science*. At http://www.ucsusa.org.

UN News Centre. 2007. "Preference for Sons in Asia Could Have Severe Social Consequences: UN Agency." News release, October 29. At http://www.un.org/apps/news/story.asp?NewsID=24454&Cr=unfpa&Cr1 (accessed August 2008).

UN News Service. 2008. "BBC to Broadcast UN-Funded Documentary on India's Preference for Sons." August 13. UNHCR Refworld. At http://www.unhcr.org/refworld/docid/48b287cf1e.html (accessed April 18, 2009).

U.S. Environmental Protection Agency. 2008. "The Presidential Green Chemistry Challenge." At http://www.epa.gov/gcc/pubs/pgcc/presgcc.html (accessed July 11, 2008).

U.S. House of Representatives. 2003. *Politics and Science in the Bush Administration*. Committee on Government Reform, Minority Staff. Washington, D.C. At http://www.house.gov/reform/min/politicsandscience/.

Valian, Virginia. 1998. *Why So Slow? The Advancement of Women*. Cambridge, Mass.: MIT Press.

——. 2005. *Tutorials for Change: Gender Schemas and Science Careers*. Retrieved November, 2009 from http://www.hunter.cuny.edu/gendertutorial/

Van Fraassen, Bas C. 1980. *The Scientific Image*. Oxford: Clarendon.

Wainberg, Mark A. 2006. "Overview: The Making of an Era." *Seed* 2, no. 6: 57.

Wanjiku, Joy. 2006. "Money: The Swindler, Kenya." *Seed* 2, no. 6: 64.

Waring, Marilyn J. 1992. "Economics." In Cheris Kramarae and Dale Spender, eds., *The Knowledge Explosion*. New York and London: Teachers College Press, 303–309.

——. 1997. *Three Masquerades: Essays on Equity, Work, and Hu(man) Rights*. Toronto: University of Toronto Press.

Wartofsky, Marx W. 1996. "Positivism and Politics: The Vienna Circle as a Social Movement." In Sahotra Sarkar, ed., *The Legacy of the Vienna Circle: Modern Reappraisals*. New York and London: Garland, 53–75.

Watson, Patty Jo, and Mary C. Kennedy. 1991. "The Development of Horticulture in the Eastern Woodlands of North America: Women's Role." In Joan M. Gero and Margaret W. Conkey, eds., *Engendering Archaeology: Women and Prehistory*. Oxford and Cambridge, Mass.: Basil Blackwell, 255–275.

Weisman, Carol S., and Sandra D. Cassard. 1994. "Health Consequences of Exclusion or Underrepresentation of Women in Clinical Studies (I)." In Anna C. Mastroianni, Ruth Faden, and Daniel Federman, eds., *Women and Health Research*, vol. 2. Washington, D.C.: National Academy Press, 35–40.

Wells, Frank, and Michael Farthing. 2008. *Fraud and Misconduct in Biomedical Research*, 4th ed. London: Royal Society of Medicine.

West, Carolyn. 2002. "Black Battered Women: New Directions for Research and Black Feminist Theory." In Lynn Collins, Michelle Dunlap, and Joan Chrisler, eds., *Charting a New Course for Feminist Psychology*. Westport, Conn.: Praeger, 216–237.

——, ed. 2004. *Violence in the Lives of Black Women: Battered, Black, and Blue*. New York: Haworth.

West, Martha S., and John W. Curtis. 2006. *AAUP Faculty Gender Equity Indicators 2006*. Washington, D.C.: American Association of University Professors. At http://www.aaup.org/NR/rdonlyres/63396944–44BE-4ABA-9815–5792D93856F1/0/AAUPGenderEquityIndicators2006.pdf (accessed June 5, 2008).

Westfall, Richard S. 1989. *Essays on the Trial of Galileo*. Vatican City: Vatican Observatory.

Wheeler, Carolynne. 2006. "Conflict: The Security Threat, Palestine." *Seed* 2, no. 6: 63.

Wilholt, Torsten. Forthcoming. "Scientific Freedom: Its Grounds and Their Limitations." *Studies in History and Philosophy of Science*.

Wilkie, Laurie. 2003. *The Archaeology of Mothering: An African-American Midwife's Tale*. London: Routledge.

Wilkinson, Sue. 1997. "Still Seeking Transformation: Feminist Challenges to Psychology." In Liz Stanley, ed., *Knowing Feminisms: On Academic Borders, Territories and Tribes*. London: Sage, 97–108.

Wohn, D. Yvette, and Dennis Normile. 2006. "Hwang Indicted for Fraud, Embezzlement." *Science NOW Daily News* (May 12). At http://sciencenow.sciencemag.org/cgi/content/full/2006/512/1.

"Women's Health Research." 1995. *Science* 269: 765–801.

World Congress for Freedom of Scientific Research. 2009. "From the Body to the Body Politic." Second Meeting of the World Congress for Freedom of Scientific Research, Brussels, March 5–7, 2009. Program at http://www.freedomofresearch.org/files/Progr_World_Congress_FINAL!.pdf Video at http://www.freedomof-research.org/ (accessed December 26, 2009)

Wylie, Alison. 1996. "Ethical Dilemmas in Archaeological Practice: Looting, Repatriation, Stewardship, and the (Trans)formation of Disciplinary Identity." *Perspectives on Science* 4, no. 2: 154–194.

———. 1997. "The Engendering of Archaeology: Refiguring Feminist Science Studies." In Sally Kohlstedt and Helen Longino, eds., *Women, Gender, and Science: New Directions, Osiris* 12: 80–99.

———. 1999. "Science, Conservation, and Stewardship: Evolving Codes of Conduct in Archaeology." *Science and Engineering Ethics* 5: 319–336.

———. 2001. "Doing Social Science as a Feminist: The Engendering of Archeology." In Angela N. Creager, Elizabeth Lunbeck, and Londa Schiebinger, eds., *Feminism in Twentieth-Century Science, Technology, and Medicine*. Chicago: University of Chicago Press, 23–45.

———. 2003. "Why Standpoint Matters." In Robert Figueroa and Sandra Harding, eds., *Science and Other Cultures: Issues in Philosophies of Science and Technology*. New York and London: Routledge.

———. 2005. "The Promise and Perils of an Ethic of Stewardship." In Lynn Meskell and Peter Pels, eds., *Embedding Ethics*. Oxford: Berg, 47–68.

———. 2007. "The Feminism Question in Science: What Does It Mean to 'Do Social Science as a Feminist'?" In Sharlene Nagy Hesse-Biber, ed., *Handbook of Feminist Research: Theory and Praxis*. Thousand Oaks, Calif.: Sage.

Wylie, Alison, and Lynn Hankinson Nelson. 2007. "Coming to Terms with the Values of Science: Insights from Feminist Science Studies Scholarship." In Harold Kincaid, John Dupré , and Alison Wylie, eds., *Value-Free Science? Ideals and Illusions*. New York: Oxford University Press.

Wylie, Alison, Janet R. Jakobsen, and Gisela Fosado. 2007. *Women, Work, and the Academy: Strategies for Responding to "Post-Civil Rights Era" Gender Discrimination*. New York: Barnard Center for Research on Women. At http://feministphiloso-phers.files.wordpress.com/2008/01/bcrw-womenworkacademy_08.pdf (accessed February 24, 2008).

Ziman, John. 2000a. "Postacademic Science: Constructing Knowledge with Networks and Norms." In Ullica Segerstrale, ed., *Beyond the Science Wars: The Missing Discourse about Science and Society*. Albany: State University of New York Press, 135–154.

———. 2000b. *Real Science: What It Is, and What It Means*. Cambridge: Cambridge University Press.

Zuckerman, Harriet. 1988. "The Sociology of Science." In Neil J. Smelser, ed., *Handbook of Sociology*. Newbury Park, Calif.: Sage, 511–574.

Index